PLANT-BASED
QUICK &EASY
COOKBOOK

GARDEN of GRAPES.

First Edition: 2023

Published by Garden of Grapes.

Printed in USA

The recipes, techniques, and tips in this cookbook are intended for personal use only. The author and publisher are not responsible for any adverse effects or consequences resulting from the use of the recipes or suggestions in this book.

Library of Congress Cataloging-in-Publication Data:

First edition.
Includes index.

Manufactured in USA

Introduction

Ladies and gentlemen, fellow food enthusiasts,

Welcome to the vibrant world of plant-based cuisine, a realm where flavors dance, colors pop, and nourishment thrives. As we embark on this culinary adventure through the pages of "Plant-Based Quick and Easy Cookbook: Fast, Healthy, and Delicious," I extend to you a warm and hearty welcome.

In this cookbook, we delve into a theme that resonates with the busy, health-conscious, and taste-loving individuals of today: the art of fast, healthy, and delectable plant-based cooking. Our goal is to empower you with the knowledge and inspiration to master the art of creating wholesome, plant-based dishes that not only fuel your body but also tantalize your taste buds.

What inspired me to bring this cookbook to life, you might wonder? It's the sheer delight of crafting dishes that are a celebration of nature's bounty. It's the gratification of knowing that every meal we prepare can be a step towards improved well-being, both for ourselves and the planet. It's the belief that plant-based cooking can be convenient without sacrificing flavor and nutrition.

In the following pages, you can expect to find a treasure trove of recipes that are not only easy to prepare but also bursting with goodness. These recipes are designed to be your allies in the kitchen, your companions on your journey to a healthier lifestyle. Whether you're a seasoned plant-based chef or a newcomer to this exciting culinary landscape, there's something for everyone.

Our repertoire covers a diverse range of culinary creations, from quick and nutritious breakfasts that kickstart your day to satisfying and fulfilling dinners that cap it off perfectly. You'll discover innovative salads that redefine what it means to eat your greens, hearty soups that comfort your soul, and globally inspired dishes that transport your taste buds to far-off places.

As you flip through the pages, you'll find step-by-step guidance, along with vivid pictures that bring these recipes to life. The beauty of plant-based cooking lies not just in the flavors but also in the colors, and our images are a testament to the visual delight that awaits you in your kitchen.

So, without further ado, let's embark on this journey of culinary discovery. Let the delectable aromas and sumptuous flavors of plant-based cuisine fill your kitchen. With each page turned and every dish prepared, you'll be one step closer to mastering the art of plant-based cooking, all while enjoying fast, healthy, and delicious meals.

Thank you for choosing "Plant-Based Quick and Easy Cookbook." May your culinary adventures be as joyful and satisfying as the recipes themselves.

To your health and culinary exploration,

Garden of Grapes

Cooking Philosophy or Approach

Ladies and gentlemen, let's delve into the culinary philosophy that defines the heart and soul of the "Plant-Based Quick and Easy Cookbook." This is more than just a collection of recipes; it's a journey into the art of nourishing our bodies and delighting our taste buds with vibrant, plant-based creations.

Our Approach to Cooking and Food:

At the core of our cookbook lies a profound respect for the bountiful offerings of nature. We believe that whole, plant-based foods are a treasure trove of flavors, textures, and nutrients. They're not just ingredients; they're our allies in creating mouthwatering dishes that also contribute to our well-being.

Our approach to cooking is rooted in simplicity and accessibility. We understand that the demands of modern life can be daunting, leaving little time for intricate culinary endeavors. That's why we've designed our recipes with a focus on speed and ease. In this cookbook, you'll discover a world of possibilities that can be realized without spending hours in the kitchen.

We embrace the idea that cooking is an art form, and like any art, it should be a joyful experience. Cooking should be a source of creativity, not stress. Our recipes reflect this ethos by emphasizing straightforward techniques that anyone can master. You won't need a vast array of specialized kitchen gadgets or exotic ingredients; just a willingness to explore and a desire to savor the goodness of plant-based cuisine.

Techniques, Ingredients, and Styles:

In these pages, you'll encounter a diverse range of cooking techniques. From the simplicity of sautéing and roasting to the artistry of plating and garnishing, our recipes cover the spectrum. We believe that every culinary skill you acquire is a tool in your kitchen repertoire, and we're here to help you build that repertoire.

As for ingredients, we put an emphasis on whole foods. Fresh vegetables, fruits, grains, legumes, and nuts are the stars of our show. You'll see how these ingredients can be combined in myriad ways to create everything from hearty mains to delectable desserts. We also appreciate the role of herbs, spices, and seasonings in elevating flavors. You'll become acquainted with various flavor profiles, from the warmth of Mediterranean spices to the boldness of Asian seasoning.

Our styles of cooking are inspired by cuisines from around the globe. You'll find dishes influenced by the vibrant spices of Indian cuisine, the simplicity of Mediterranean cooking, the umami-rich creations of Japanese fare, and so much more. We believe that diversity is the spice of life, and it certainly adds a world of excitement to your plant-based meals.

In conclusion, our cookbook is a celebration of the plant-based journey, from the soil to the plate. It's a testament to the idea that cooking should be enjoyable, nourishing, and accessible to everyone. So, whether you're a seasoned home cook or a kitchen novice, we invite you to embrace the world of plant-based cuisine with open arms and an open heart.

Here's to quick, healthy, and delicious plant-based cooking that will not only satiate your taste buds but also nurture your body and spirit.

Vegan Quesadillas
See page, 63

Tips for Successful Cooking

Ladies and gentlemen, comrades in the culinary journey,

I'm not here to tell you that life-altering, awe-inspiring plant-based dishes require a three-hour prep time, a handful of obscure ingredients, or a culinary degree. No, no. We're here to celebrate the art of quick and easy plant-based cooking. I'm talking about vibrant, tantalizing, and downright delectable dishes that will leave your taste buds cheering, all while saving you precious time and effort. So, let's dive into some tips and techniques that'll make your plant-based culinary adventures smooth sailing.

1. Master the Art of Mise en Place: This French term essentially means "everything in its place." Before you even think about turning on the stove, ensure your ingredients are chopped, measured, and ready to roll. It's like having your own support team right there on the countertop, making the cooking process feel effortless.

2. Embrace the Rainbow: The more colors on your plate, the better. A variety of vegetables not only looks stunning but also packs a diverse nutritional punch. Think red bell peppers, leafy greens, vibrant carrots – the works. The more colorful your ingredients, the more antioxidants you'll get.

3. Spice It Up: Don't be shy with the spices. Fresh herbs, dried spices, and seasonings are your secret weapons. Elevate your dishes with a pinch of this and a dash of that. If you're new to spices, experiment to discover your favorites.

4. Create Flavorful Bases: Stock up on canned tomatoes, vegetable broth, coconut milk, and other flavor-rich bases. These will be your go-to for quick sauces, soups, and stews.

5. Know Your Substitutes: Plant-based cooking often involves substituting animal products with plant alternatives. Think tofu, tempeh, or seitan instead of meat. Nutritional yeast can provide that cheesy flavor, and cashew cream makes an excellent dairy alternative. The world of plant-based swaps is vast; explore it.

6. Get Comfy with One-Pot and Sheet Pan Meals:
Let's keep the cleanup simple. One-pot and sheet
pan recipes are not only time-savers but also flavor
enhancers. The ingredients cozy up together,
creating a delightful medley of flavors with minimal
effort.

7. Batch Cooking is Your Friend: Cook once, eat
twice, or even thrice. Making larger portions and
freezing or refrigerating the extras is a smart move.
It means that when life gets hectic, you have a
plant-based meal just minutes away.

8. Taste As You Go: Unlike baking, cooking is a
realm where you can tweak and adjust as you go.
Taste your dish at various stages and adjust
seasonings to your liking. Remember, you're the
boss in the kitchen.

9. Knife Skills Matter: Whether you're dicing,
chopping, or julienning, knife skills can save you a
lot of time. Sharpen those blades and practice your
cuts. It'll make the prep work a breeze.

10. Don't Fear Frozen Fruits and Veggies: Fresh is
fantastic, but don't underestimate the power of
frozen produce. They're convenient, nutrient-
packed, and readily available year-round.

Now, as we embark on this whirlwind adventure of
flavor and convenience, remember that cooking is
an expression of creativity and love. You're crafting
not just meals but memories. So, dive into the
vibrant world of plant-based quick and easy
cooking, and let your culinary spirit run wild.

Happy cooking!

Yours in flavor and haste,
Garden of Grapes

Vegan Philly Cheesesteak
See page, 65

Kitchen Essentials

Alright, my fellow culinary explorers, before we set sail on this plant-based adventure, let's talk about the unsung heroes of the kitchen—the tools and equipment that will transform your cooking from a mundane task into an artful experience.

In your journey through the "Plant-Based Quick and Easy Cookbook: Fast, Healthy, and Delicious," you'll discover the pure delight of creating scrumptious dishes. To make this journey a breeze, you'll want to arm yourself with the right kitchen essentials. So, let's dive in and discuss the must-haves and how to wield them with finesse.

Essential Kitchen Tools and Equipment:

1. Sharp Chef's Knife: This kitchen knight is your trusty sidekick. It's the difference between a graceful julienne and a haphazard chop. Keep it sharp, and it'll serve you well.

2. Cutting Board: A good-sized, sturdy cutting board provides a stable platform for your culinary artistry. Whether it's slicing, dicing, or chopping, your cutting board has your back.

3. Vegetable Peeler: A reliable peeler is indispensable for prepping your veggies. It's the key to unlocking the flavors within those skins.

4. Pots and Pans: Invest in a few quality pots and pans. You'll need various sizes for boiling, sautéing, and simmering. A non-stick pan is great for minimizing the use of oil.

5. Baking Sheets: For those delightful roasted veggies or golden-brown fries, a sturdy baking sheet is a must. Make sure to line it with parchment paper or a silicone baking mat for easy cleanup.

6. Blender: When it comes to silky smooth soups, velvety sauces, or satisfying smoothies, a high-speed blender is your go-to. It's a magician in disguise.

7. Food Processor: A food processor is your culinary multitool. It can chop, slice, shred, and even knead dough. Your sous chef in electronic form.

8. Measuring Cups and Spoons: Precision is key in cooking, and these tools are your navigational instruments. They ensure your culinary ship stays on course.

9. Mixing Bowls: A variety of mixing bowls in different sizes will come in handy for preparing ingredients and dressings. They're the canvas for your culinary creations.

Tips on How to Use These Tools Effectively:

- Knife Skills: Take the time to hone your knife skills. A well-sharpened chef's knife, combined with proper technique, will make your prep work a breeze. Practice your "claw" hand to protect your fingers while cutting.

- Storage: Keep your knives sharp by storing them properly. Magnetic strips or knife blocks are ideal. And always wash them by hand to maintain their edge.

- Blender Mastery: When using your blender, start with liquids, then add soft ingredients, and finish with the harder ones. This ensures a smoother blend.

- Food Processor Finesse: Avoid overfilling your food processor. Work in batches if necessary. And when chopping, use short pulses to control the consistency of the chop.

- Baking Sheets: To prevent sticking and simplify cleaning, line your baking sheets with parchment paper or silicone mats before roasting or baking.

- Maintain Your Equipment: Regularly check and maintain your tools. A well-cared-for kitchen is a happy kitchen.

With these kitchen essentials and the knowledge of how to wield them skillfully, you're all set to embark on your plant-based culinary adventure. So, let's get cooking and create the delicious, healthy, and fast dishes that await in the pages of our cookbook.

Bon appétit, my friends! 🍴

Vegan Caesar Salad
See page, 14

Flavor Pairing Suggestions

Flavor Pairing Suggestions: Unleash Your Culinary Creativity

Alright, my fellow culinary adventurers, we've journeyed through the pages of the "Plant-Based Quick and Easy Cookbook," discovering the art of crafting fast, healthy, and downright delicious plant-based dishes. But before we bid adieu to this flavor-packed expedition, I've got a little gift for you. a secret to unleash your inner chef.

One of the greatest joys in cooking is experimenting, mixing, and matching flavors to create something entirely new. It's like a painter with an infinite palette, and today, I'm here to provide you with the colors. In this section, we're talking about flavor pairing suggestions.

As we've explored throughout the cookbook, the world of plant-based ingredients is a vast one, teeming with an array of tastes, textures, and aromas. The magic truly happens when you find the right combinations, the duets that can turn an ordinary dish into a masterpiece. So, here are some ideas to get those creative gears turning:

1. Lemony Freshness: When you want to add a zesty punch to your dishes, think of pairing lemon with greens, like arugula or spinach. Drizzle it over roasted veggies for a citrusy delight.

2. Creamy and Nutty: Creaminess meets nuttiness in a beautiful embrace. Try blending cashews with butternut squash for a velvety soup. It's a match made in culinary heaven.

3. Earthy Harmony: Root vegetables and herbs are like old friends. Think of the earthy sweetness of beets combined with the fresh vibrancy of rosemary or thyme.

4. Spicy Allure: For those who like a kick, the marriage of cayenne and dark chocolate is divine. A spicy chocolate sauce drizzled over fruit will tantalize your taste buds.

5. Mediterranean Melody: Tomatoes and basil, the classic Mediterranean pair. Roasted tomatoes with a generous sprinkle of fresh basil leaves - it's like summer on a plate.

6. Tropical Dreams: Sweet pineapple and savory cilantro - it's a tropical dance of flavors. Try it in a salsa alongside grilled tofu or tempeh.

7. Savory Elegance: Sage, known for its deep, earthy aroma, pairs beautifully with the mellow elegance of mushrooms. Sage-infused oil drizzled over a mushroom risotto? Yes, please.

8. Asian Fusion: Ginger and garlic are like the dynamic duo of Asian cuisine. They add that unmistakable depth of flavor to stir-fries and sauces.

Now, remember, these suggestions are merely the starting point of your own culinary adventures. The real magic happens when you combine these ideas, follow your instincts, and let your taste buds guide the way. After all, cooking is an art, and you are the artist.

So, the next time you stand before your kitchen canvas, armed with ingredients, pots, and pans, don't forget to channel your inner artist. Experiment, create, and relish the delightful surprises that await you. That's the true essence of cooking, and that's where the magic happens.

Thank you for embarking on this flavorful journey with me. Until we meet again in the realm of culinary exploration, keep those pots sizzling and those taste buds tingling.

Yours in flavor and adventure,
Garden of Grapes

INDEX

Chapter 1:
Morning Boosts

2
pancakes

150

15 min

Vegan Banana Pancakes

Ingredients:

- 1 ripe banana
- 1 cup flour
- 1 tbsp sugar
- 1 tsp baking powder
- 1/2 tsp cinnamon
- 1 cup almond milk
- 1 tsp vanilla extract

Substitutions

- Use maple syrup instead of sugar for a different sweetness.
- Almond milk can be replaced with any plant-based milk.

These fluffy pancakes are a vegan twist on a classic favorite. Enjoy the sweet aroma of ripe bananas in every bite.

Directions

1. Mash the banana in a bowl.
2. In a separate bowl, mix flour, sugar, baking powder, and cinnamon.
3. Add almond milk and vanilla extract to the mashed banana.
4. Combine wet and dry ingredients until smooth.
5. Cook pancakes on a hot griddle until golden brown on both sides.
6. Serve with maple syrup and fresh fruit.

2 servings   **180**   **20 min**

Tofu Scramble

Ingredients:

- 1 block tofu, crumbled
- 1/2 onion, diced
- 1/2 bell pepper, diced
- 1/2 tsp turmeric
- 1/2 tsp cumin
- Salt and pepper to taste
- Spinach leaves
- 2 tbsp nutritional yeast

A protein-packed delight, this tofu scramble will make you forget all about eggs. Perfect for a hearty breakfast.

Directions

1. Sauté onions and bell pepper until soft.
2. Add crumbled tofu and cook until slightly browned.
3. Sprinkle turmeric, cumin, salt, and pepper.
4. Stir in spinach and nutritional yeast.
5. Cook until spinach wilts.
6. Serve hot.

Substitutions

- Add diced tomatoes for extra flavor.
- Substitute nutritional yeast with vegan cheese shreds.

2 toasts   220   10 min

Avocado Toast with Chickpea Mash

Ingredients:

- 2 slices of whole-grain bread
- 1 ripe avocado
- 1/2 cup canned chickpeas, drained
- 1/2 lemon, juiced
- Salt and pepper to taste

Substitutions

- Add sliced tomatoes or cucumber for freshness.
- Try different types of bread for variety.

Creamy avocado meets zesty chickpea mash on crispy toast. A simple yet sensational breakfast that's ready in a flash.

Directions

1. Mash chickpeas with lemon juice, salt, and pepper.
2. Spread mashed avocado on toasted bread.
3. Top with chickpea mash.
4. Drizzle with olive oil, if desired.
5. Sprinkle with red pepper flakes for a kick.

2
burritos

280

25 min

Vegan Breakfast Burritos

Ingredients:

- 2 large tortillas
- 1 cup tofu scramble (from previous recipe)
- 1/2 cup black beans, cooked
- Salsa
- Avocado slices
- Spinach leaves

These burritos are packed with goodness – tofu scramble, black beans, and veggies wrapped in a tortilla. A portable breakfast fiesta!

Directions

1. Warm tortillas in a pan.
2. Fill each tortilla with tofu scramble, black beans, salsa, avocado, and spinach.
3. Fold into a burrito.
4. Grill until golden brown.
5. Serve with extra salsa.

Substitutions

- Add vegan cheese for a melty twist.
- Customize with your favorite veggies.

1 serving | 250 | 10 min

Blueberry Oatmeal

Ingredients:

- 1/2 cup rolled oats
- 1 cup almond milk
- 1/2 cup blueberries
- 1 tbsp maple syrup
- 1/2 tsp vanilla extract
- Pinch of salt

A comforting bowl of oatmeal with bursts of juicy blueberries. It's like a hug in a bowl to start your day right.

Directions

1. Combine oats, almond milk, and salt in a saucepan.
2. Cook over medium heat until creamy.
3. Stir in blueberries, maple syrup, and vanilla extract.
4. Cook for an additional 2 minutes.
5. Serve hot.

Substitutions

- Swap blueberries with your favorite berries.
- Add a dollop of almond butter for extra richness.

2
servings

180

5 min

Chia Pudding with Berries

Ingredients:

- 1/4 cup chia seeds
- 1 cup almond milk
- 1 tbsp maple syrup
- 1/2 tsp vanilla extract
- Mixed berries for topping

Chia seeds magically transform into a creamy pudding overnight. Top with fresh berries for a burst of flavor.

Directions

1. Mix chia seeds, almond milk, maple syrup, and vanilla extract in a jar.
2. Refrigerate overnight or for at least 4 hours.
3. Stir well before serving.
4. Top with mixed berries.

Substitutions

- Customize with your favorite toppings like nuts or coconut flakes.
- Use any sweetener of your choice.

2
servings

200

20 min

Vegan French Toast

Ingredients:

- 4 slices of bread
- 1/2 cup almond milk
- 2 tbsp flour
- 1 tsp vanilla extract
- 1/2 tsp cinnamon
- Pinch of salt
- Maple syrup for drizzling

Crispy on the outside, tender on the inside – this vegan French toast is a breakfast classic reimagined for everyone to enjoy.

Directions

1. In a bowl, whisk almond milk, flour, vanilla extract, cinnamon, and salt.
2. Dip bread slices in the mixture, coating both sides.
3. Cook on a hot griddle until golden brown.
4. Drizzle with maple syrup.
5. Serve with fresh fruit.

Substitutions

- Add a dash of nutmeg for extra flavor.
- Top with vegan whipped cream for a decadent treat.

2 servings   **280**   **15 min**

Breakfast Quinoa Bowl

Ingredients:

- 1 cup cooked quinoa
- 1/2 cup almond milk
- 1/2 cup mixed berries
- 2 tbsp chopped nuts (e.g., almonds, walnuts)
- 1 tbsp honey

Power up your morning with this quinoa bowl loaded with fruits, nuts, and a drizzle of honey. A breakfast that's as nutritious as it is delicious.

Directions

1. In a bowl, combine quinoa and almond milk.
2. Top with mixed berries and chopped nuts.
3. Drizzle with honey.
4. Enjoy warm.

Substitutions

- Use any type of milk you prefer.
- Customize with your favorite fruits and nuts.

2 servings   **220** kcal   **30 min**

Sweet Potato and Black Bean Breakfast Hash

Ingredients:

- 2 medium sweet potatoes, diced
- 1 can black beans, drained and rinsed
- 1/2 onion, diced
- 1 red bell pepper, diced
- 1 tsp cumin
- 1/2 tsp paprika
- Salt and pepper to taste

This savory hash is a delightful blend of sweet potatoes, black beans, and spices. It's a hearty breakfast that's bursting with flavors.

Directions

1. Heat oil in a skillet and sauté onions and bell pepper until soft.
2. Add sweet potatoes and cook until they begin to brown.
3. Stir in black beans, cumin, paprika, salt, and pepper.
4. Cook until sweet potatoes are tender.
5. Serve hot.

Substitutions

- Top with avocado slices or salsa for extra flair.
- Add some vegan cheese for a melty twist.

1 serving   200   10 min

Green Smoothie Bowl

This vibrant green smoothie bowl is a nutrient-packed powerhouse. It's the ultimate way to kickstart your day with a burst of energy.

Ingredients:

- 1 cup spinach
- 1/2 banana
- 1/2 avocado
- 1/2 cup almond milk
- 1 tbsp chia seeds
- Toppings: sliced banana, granola, berries

Directions

1. Blend spinach, banana, avocado, and almond milk until smooth.
2. Pour into a bowl and top with chia seeds, sliced banana, granola, and berries.
3. Enjoy your green goodness.

Substitutions

- Customize with your favorite toppings and greens.
- Add a drizzle of honey or maple syrup for sweetness.

Chapter 2:
Lunchtime
Satisfiers

2
sandwic
hes

280

15 min

Chickpea Salad Sandwich

Ingredients:

- 1 can chickpeas, drained and mashed
- 1/4 cup vegan mayo
- 1/4 cup diced celery
- 1/4 cup diced red onion
- 2 tbsp chopped fresh dill
- Salt and pepper to taste
- 4 slices of whole-grain bread

A wholesome and protein-packed delight, this chickpea salad sandwich is a perfect lunchtime treat.

Directions

1. In a bowl, mix mashed chickpeas, vegan mayo, celery, red onion, and dill.
2. Season with salt and pepper.
3. Spread the chickpea salad on bread slices to make sandwiches.
4. Enjoy!

Substitutions

- Add lettuce or spinach leaves for extra freshness.
- Use avocado slices instead of mayo for creaminess.

2 servings · **230** kcal · **20 min**

Vegan Caesar Salad

Ingredients:

- 1 head romaine lettuce, chopped
- Vegan Caesar dressing
- Vegan croutons
- Vegan Parmesan cheese (optional)

Crispy romaine lettuce, tangy Caesar dressing, and crunchy croutons come together in this vegan twist on a classic Caesar salad.

Directions

1. Toss chopped romaine lettuce with vegan Caesar dressing until well coated.
2. Top with croutons and vegan Parmesan cheese, if desired.
3. Serve and enjoy!

Substitutions

- Add cherry tomatoes or roasted chickpeas for extra flavor.
- Make your own croutons by toasting bread cubes with olive oil and herbs.

2
sandwic
hes

260

15 min

Vegan BLT Sandwich

Ingredients:

- 8 slices of whole-grain bread
- 1 package tempeh bacon
- Lettuce leaves
- Sliced tomatoes
- Vegan mayo
- Mustard

Get ready for a flavor explosion with this vegan BLT sandwich. Smoky tempeh bacon, fresh lettuce, and juicy tomatoes make it a lunchtime favorite.

Directions

1. Cook tempeh bacon in a pan until crispy.
2. Toast bread slices.
3. Spread vegan mayo and mustard on the bread.
4. Assemble sandwiches with tempeh bacon, lettuce, and tomato slices.
5. Enjoy!

Substitutions

- Add avocado slices for extra creaminess.
- Use spinach or arugula instead of lettuce for a peppery kick.

2 servings **260** **20 min**

Greek Quinoa Salad

Ingredients:

- 1 cup cooked quinoa
- 1/2 cup cucumber, diced
- 1/2 cup cherry tomatoes, halved
- 1/4 cup Kalamata olives, pitted and sliced
- 1/4 cup red onion, finely chopped
- Vegan feta cheese (optional)
- Greek dressing

This Greek quinoa salad is a burst of Mediterranean flavors with olives, cucumbers, tomatoes, and a zesty dressing.

Directions

1. In a bowl, combine cooked quinoa, cucumber, cherry tomatoes, Kalamata olives, and red onion.
2. Drizzle with Greek dressing and toss to coat.
3. Top with vegan feta cheese, if desired.
4. Serve chilled.

Substitutions

- Customize with your favorite Mediterranean ingredients like artichoke hearts or roasted red peppers.
- Make your own Greek dressing with olive oil, lemon juice, garlic, and oregano.

2
servings

320

25 min

Spicy Thai Noodle Salad

Ingredients:

- 6 oz rice noodles, cooked and cooled
- 1/4 cup peanut butter
- 2 tbsp soy sauce
- 1 tbsp Sriracha sauce (adjust to taste)
- 1 tbsp lime juice
- 1 tsp sesame oil
- 1 cup mixed vegetables (carrots, bell peppers, and cucumber)
- Fresh cilantro and crushed peanuts for garnish

Dive into a bowl of spicy Thai noodle salad with a symphony of flavors and textures. It's a taste of Southeast Asia in every bite.

Directions

1. In a bowl, whisk together peanut butter, soy sauce, Sriracha, lime juice, and sesame oil to make the dressing.
2. Toss cooked rice noodles and mixed vegetables with the dressing.
3. Garnish with fresh cilantro and crushed peanuts.
4. Enjoy the spicy goodness!

Substitutions

- Add tofu or tempeh for extra protein.
- Customize the level of spiciness to your preference.

2 wraps | 240 | 15 min

Veggie Wrap with Hummus

Ingredients:

- 2 large whole-grain wraps
- 1/2 cup hummus
- Sliced cucumber
- Sliced bell peppers
- Sliced avocado
- Baby spinach leaves
- Sliced red onion

These veggie wraps are a medley of colors and flavors, filled with fresh vegetables and creamy hummus.

Directions

1. Lay out the wraps and spread hummus evenly on each.
2. Layer with cucumber, bell peppers, avocado, spinach, and red onion.
3. Roll up the wraps and cut in half.
4. Enjoy your portable veggie delight!

Substitutions

- Use any of your favorite veggies for customization.
- Add a drizzle of balsamic glaze for extra flavor.

2
servings

350

30 min

Vegan Buddha Bowl

Ingredients:

- 1 cup cooked quinoa
- Mixed greens
- Roasted sweet potato cubes
- Steamed broccoli florets
- Sliced carrots
- Chickpeas, roasted with spices
- Tahini dressing

This Buddha bowl is a work of art, combining grains, greens, and a rainbow of vegetables, topped with a tahini dressing.

Directions

1. In each bowl, layer cooked quinoa, mixed greens, sweet potato cubes, broccoli, carrots, and roasted chickpeas.
2. Drizzle with tahini dressing.
3. Serve and savor the flavors.

Substitutions

- Add avocado or roasted cauliflower for extra variety.
- Substitute tahini dressing with your favorite vegan dressing.

2
servings

280

35 min

Roasted Vegetable and Quinoa Bowl

Ingredients:

- 1 cup cooked quinoa
- Assorted roasted vegetables (e.g., bell peppers, zucchini, cherry tomatoes)
- Vegan pesto sauce
- Pine nuts for garnish

A hearty and nutritious bowl featuring roasted vegetables, quinoa, and a savory sauce. A wholesome lunch that's worth savoring.

Directions

1. In each bowl, layer cooked quinoa and roasted vegetables.
2. Drizzle with vegan pesto sauce.
3. Garnish with pine nuts.
4. Enjoy this rustic delight.

Substitutions

- Use your favorite roasted veggies or seasonal produce.
- Try different nut or seed garnishes for added texture.

2 rolls | 250 kcal | 30 min

Vegan Sushi Rolls

Ingredients:

- Nori seaweed sheets
- Sushi rice, seasoned with rice vinegar and sugar
- Sliced avocado
- Sliced cucumber
- Sliced bell peppers
- Carrot strips
- Soy sauce and wasabi for dipping

Substitutions

- Customize fillings with your favorite vegetables or tofu.
- Experiment with different dipping sauces for variety.

Roll up your sleeves and create these delightful vegan sushi rolls with colorful veggies and creamy avocado.

Directions

1. Place a bamboo sushi rolling mat on a clean surface, covered with plastic wrap.
2. Lay a sheet of nori, shiny side down, on the mat.
3. Spread a thin layer of sushi rice over the nori, leaving a small border.
4. Arrange avocado, cucumber, bell peppers, and carrots in the center.
5. Roll tightly, using the mat to shape the roll.
6. Slice into bite-sized pieces.
7. Serve with soy sauce and wasabi.
8. Enjoy your homemade sushi!

2 servings · **290 kcal** · **45 min**

Vegan Stuffed Bell Peppers

Ingredients:

- 2 large bell peppers, any color
- 1 cup cooked brown rice
- 1/2 cup cooked black beans
- 1/2 cup corn kernels
- 1/2 cup diced tomatoes
- 1/4 cup diced red onion
- 1/2 tsp cumin
- 1/2 tsp chili powder
- Salt and pepper to taste
- Vegan cheese for topping (optional)

These bell peppers are stuffed with a savory mix of rice, vegetables, and spices, baked to perfection. A comforting and wholesome lunch.

Directions

1. Preheat the oven to 375°F (190°C).
2. Cut the tops off the bell peppers and remove seeds.
3. In a bowl, combine cooked brown rice, black beans, corn, diced tomatoes, red onion, cumin, chili powder, salt, and pepper.
4. Stuff each bell pepper with the rice mixture.
5. Place stuffed peppers in a baking dish.
6. Cover with foil and bake for 30-35 minutes, or until peppers are tender.
7. If desired, sprinkle with vegan cheese during the last 5 minutes of baking.
8. Serve hot and enjoy!

Substitutions

- Add a drizzle of hot sauce for some heat.
- Customize the filling with your favorite spices and veggies.

Chapter 3:
Dinner Delights

4
servings

300

25 min

Vegan Chickpea Curry

Ingredients:

- 2 cans chickpeas, drained
- 1 onion, chopped
- 2 cloves garlic, minced
- 1 can diced tomatoes
- 1 can coconut milk
- 2 tbsp curry powder
- 1 tsp cumin
- 1 tsp coriander
- Salt and pepper to taste

This vegan chickpea curry is a warm and comforting dish filled with aromatic spices and tender chickpeas. A dinner that's both flavorful and nourishing.

Directions

1. In a large pot, sauté chopped onion and garlic until fragrant.
2. Add chickpeas and cook for a few minutes.
3. Stir in diced tomatoes, coconut milk, curry powder, cumin, coriander, salt, and pepper.
4. Simmer for 15-20 minutes, or until the curry thickens and flavors meld.
5. Serve with rice or naan.
6. Enjoy your homemade curry!

Substitutions

- Add spinach or other greens for extra nutrients.
- Customize the spice level to your liking.
- Use light coconut milk for a lighter version.

4
servings

280

30 min

Mushroom and Spinach Stroganoff

Creamy and savory, this vegan mushroom and spinach stroganoff is a delightful twist on a classic comfort food.

Ingredients:

- 8 oz fettuccine pasta (or pasta of your choice)
- 8 oz mushrooms, sliced
- 2 cups fresh spinach
- 1 onion, diced
- 2 cloves garlic, minced
- 1 cup vegetable broth
- 1 cup cashews, soaked and blended into a creamy sauce
- 1 tsp thyme
- Salt and pepper to taste

Directions

1. Cook pasta according to package instructions.
2. In a large skillet, sauté onions and garlic until softened.
3. Add sliced mushrooms and cook until they release their moisture.
4. Pour in vegetable broth and bring to a simmer.
5. Stir in cashew cream sauce, thyme, salt, and pepper.
6. Add fresh spinach and cook until wilted.
7. Serve the stroganoff over cooked pasta.
8. Enjoy the creamy goodness!

Substitutions

- Use any type of pasta you prefer.
- Substitute spinach with kale or Swiss chard.
- Add a pinch of nutmeg for extra flavor.

4
servings

320

40 min

Vegan Lentil Shepherd's Pie

This vegan lentil shepherd's pie is a hearty and comforting dish filled with savory lentils and topped with creamy mashed potatoes.

Ingredients:

- 1 cup dry green or brown lentils, rinsed
- 3 cups vegetable broth
- 1 onion, diced
- 2 cloves garlic, minced
- 2 carrots, diced
- 1 cup frozen peas
- 2 tbsp tomato paste
- 1 tsp thyme
- 1 tsp rosemary
- 4 cups mashed potatoes
- Vegan butter (optional)
- Salt and pepper to taste

Directions

1. In a large pot, sauté onions and garlic until fragrant.
2. Add lentils, vegetable broth, carrots, peas, tomato paste, thyme, and rosemary.
3. Simmer for 20-25 minutes, or until lentils are tender and the mixture thickens.
4. Preheat your oven to 375°F (190°C).
5. Transfer the lentil mixture to a baking dish.
6. Spread mashed potatoes over the lentil mixture.
7. Optional: Dot the top with vegan butter.
8. Bake for 15-20 minutes, or until the top is golden brown.
9. Serve hot and enjoy!

Substitutions

- Use sweet potatoes for a twist on the mashed topping.
- Customize the vegetables with your favorites.
- Add a layer of vegan cheese for extra indulgence.

4
servings

320

30 min

Vegan Thai Red Curry

Transport your taste buds to Thailand with this rich and aromatic vegan Thai red curry. Loaded with vegetables and tofu, it's a flavorful dinner option.

Ingredients:

- 1 can coconut milk
- 2 tbsp red curry paste
- 1 block tofu, cubed
- Assorted vegetables (bell peppers, broccoli, carrots, snow peas)
- Thai basil leaves
- 1 tbsp soy sauce
- 1 tsp brown sugar
- Cooked jasmine rice for serving

Directions

1. In a large pot, simmer coconut milk and red curry paste until fragrant.
2. Add cubed tofu and cook until it absorbs the flavors.
3. Stir in assorted vegetables and cook until tender.
4. Season with soy sauce and brown sugar.
5. Add Thai basil leaves and stir.
6. Serve over cooked jasmine rice.
7. Enjoy the taste of Thailand!

Substitutions

- Customize the spice level to your liking.
- Use any combination of your favorite vegetables.
- Add a squeeze of lime juice for extra zing.

4 servings

280

35 min

Vegan Chili

Warm up your evening with a hearty bowl of vegan chili. Packed with beans, veggies, and spices, it's a comforting and satisfying dinner option.

Ingredients:

- 2 cans mixed beans (kidney beans, black beans, pinto beans), drained
- 1 can diced tomatoes
- 1 onion, diced
- 2 cloves garlic, minced
- 1 bell pepper, diced
- 1 cup corn kernels
- 2 tbsp chili powder
- 1 tsp cumin
- Salt and pepper to taste

Directions

1. In a large pot, sauté onions and garlic until fragrant.
2. Add diced tomatoes, mixed beans, bell pepper, corn, chili powder, cumin, salt, and pepper.
3. Simmer for 20-25 minutes, stirring occasionally.
4. Serve hot and garnish with your favorite toppings (avocado, vegan cheese, or cilantro).
5. Enjoy a bowl of chili goodness!

Substitutions

- Customize the spiciness with more or less chili powder.
- Add diced zucchini or sweet potatoes for extra texture.
- Serve with a side of vegan cornbread.

4
servings

260

45 min

Eggplant Parmesan

Ingredients:

- 2 large eggplants, sliced
- 2 cups marinara sauce
- 2 cups vegan mozzarella cheese
- 1 cup breadcrumbs
- 1/2 cup almond flour
- 1 tsp dried oregano
- 1 tsp dried basil
- Olive oil for frying
- Fresh basil leaves for garnish

Layers of tender eggplant, marinara sauce, and vegan cheese come together in this comforting vegan eggplant Parmesan.

Directions

1. Preheat your oven to 375°F (190°C).
2. In a shallow dish, combine breadcrumbs, almond flour, dried oregano, and dried basil.
3. Dip eggplant slices in the breadcrumb mixture to coat.
4. Heat olive oil in a skillet and fry eggplant slices until golden brown.
5. In a baking dish, layer marinara sauce, fried eggplant slices, and vegan mozzarella cheese.
6. Repeat the layers until all ingredients are used.
7. Bake for 20-25 minutes, or until the cheese is bubbly and golden.
8. Garnish with fresh basil leaves.
9. Serve hot and enjoy the comfort of eggplant Parmesan!

Substitutions

- Use gluten-free breadcrumbs for a gluten-free version.
- Add a pinch of red pepper flakes for some heat.
- Serve over cooked spaghetti for a twist.

4 servings

350 kcal

40 min

Vegan Jambalaya

Spice up your dinner with this flavorful vegan jambalaya. Packed with Cajun spices, rice, and an array of vegetables, it's a taste of Louisiana.

Ingredients:

- 1 cup long-grain rice
- 1 onion, diced
- 1 bell pepper, diced
- 2 cloves garlic, minced
- 1 cup diced tomatoes
- 1 can kidney beans, drained
- 1 cup sliced vegan sausage (e.g., andouille or Italian)
- 1 tsp Cajun seasoning
- 1/2 tsp paprika
- 1/2 tsp dried thyme
- 1/2 tsp dried oregano
- Salt and pepper to taste

Directions

1. Cook rice according to package instructions.
2. In a large skillet, sauté onions and garlic until softened.
3. Add bell pepper and cook until tender.
4. Stir in diced tomatoes, kidney beans, vegan sausage, Cajun seasoning, paprika, thyme, oregano, salt, and pepper.
5. Cook for 10-15 minutes, allowing the flavors to meld.
6. Serve over cooked rice.
7. Enjoy the spicy goodness of jambalaya!

Substitutions

- Customize the spiciness with more or less Cajun seasoning.
- Use your favorite vegan sausage or tofu for protein.
- Add sliced okra for an authentic touch.

4
servings

320

40 min

Butternut Squash and Sage Risotto

Ingredients:

- 2 cups Arborio rice
- 1/2 butternut squash, peeled and diced
- 1 onion, diced
- 2 cloves garlic, minced
- 1/2 cup dry white wine (optional)
- 6 cups vegetable broth, warmed
- Fresh sage leaves
- Vegan Parmesan cheese (optional)
- Olive oil for sautéing
- Salt and pepper to taste

Substitutions

- Use any type of winter squash for variation.
- Substitute fresh sage with dried sage.
- Add a handful of toasted pine nuts for extra crunch.

Creamy and aromatic, this vegan butternut squash and sage risotto is a comforting dinner option that's perfect for fall.

Directions

1. In a large skillet, sauté onions and garlic in olive oil until translucent.
2. Add Arborio rice and stir to coat with oil.
3. Optional: Pour in dry white wine and cook until absorbed.
4. Begin adding warmed vegetable broth one ladle at a time, stirring constantly and allowing the liquid to absorb before adding more.
5. Stir in diced butternut squash and fresh sage leaves as you continue adding broth.
6. Cook until rice is creamy and butternut squash is tender.
7. Season with salt and pepper.
8. Optional: Garnish with vegan Parmesan cheese and extra sage leaves.
9. Serve hot and savor the richness of butternut squash risotto!

4
servings

260

25 min

Vegan Tacos with Black Beans

These vegan tacos with black beans are a fiesta of flavors and textures. Fill your tortillas with spiced beans and your favorite toppings.

Ingredients:

- 1 can black beans, drained and rinsed
- 1 onion, diced
- 2 cloves garlic, minced
- 1 tsp chili powder
- 1/2 tsp cumin
- 1/2 tsp paprika
- Salt and pepper to taste
- Soft tortillas
- Toppings: sliced avocado, shredded lettuce, diced tomatoes, salsa, vegan sour cream

Directions

1. In a skillet, sauté onions and garlic until fragrant.
2. Add black beans, chili powder, cumin, paprika, salt, and pepper.
3. Cook until beans are heated through and coated in spices.
4. Warm soft tortillas.
5. Assemble tacos with spiced black beans and your choice of toppings.
6. Enjoy your vegan taco fiesta!

Substitutions

- Customize the toppings with your favorites like jalapeños or vegan cheese.
- Add a squeeze of lime juice for extra zing.
- Use crispy taco shells for a crunchy variation.

4 servings

280

30 min

Vegan BBQ Pulled Jackfruit Sandwiches

Smoky and savory, these vegan BBQ pulled jackfruit sandwiches are a delicious alternative to traditional pulled pork.

Ingredients:

- 2 cans young green jackfruit in brine, drained and shredded
- 1 onion, diced
- 2 cloves garlic, minced
- 1 cup BBQ sauce (choose your favorite vegan brand)
- Soft burger buns
- Coleslaw (optional)
- Pickles (optional)

Directions

1. In a skillet, sauté onions and garlic until softened.
2. Add shredded jackfruit and sauté for a few minutes.
3. Pour in BBQ sauce and cook until jackfruit is heated through and coated in sauce.
4. Optional: Serve on soft burger buns with coleslaw and pickles.
5. Enjoy your smoky BBQ delight!

Substitutions

- Customize the BBQ sauce to your preferred level of sweetness or spiciness.
- Add sliced jalapeños for extra heat.
- Serve with a side of sweet potato fries.

Chapter 4: Quick and Tasty Bowls

2
servings

450
calories

20 mins

Vegan Burrito Bowl

Ingredients:

- 1 cup cooked brown rice
- 1 cup black beans
- 1 cup corn kernels
- 1 cup diced tomatoes
- 1 cup sliced avocado
- 1/2 cup red onion, finely chopped
- 1/4 cup fresh cilantro, chopped
- 1 lime, juiced
- 1 tsp chili powder
- Salt and pepper to taste
- Vegan sour cream and salsa for garnish
- Tortilla chips for crunch

A fiesta in a bowl! This vegan burrito bowl is a vibrant mix of flavors and textures inspired by Mexican cuisine.

Directions

1. Cook brown rice according to package instructions.
2. In a skillet, warm black beans and corn over medium heat.
3. Mix in chili powder, salt, and pepper.
4. Assemble bowls with rice, bean mixture, tomatoes, avocado, red onion, and cilantro.
5. Drizzle with lime juice.
6. Top with vegan sour cream and salsa.
7. Serve with tortilla chips.
Enjoy your fiesta!

4 servings

380 calories

15 mins

Vegan Soba Noodle Bowl

From Japan with love! This vegan soba noodle bowl is a slurp-worthy delight, packed with umami flavors.

Ingredients:

- 8 oz soba noodles
- 1 cup edamame
- 1 cup sliced shiitake mushrooms
- 1 cup shredded carrots
- 1/4 cup sliced green onions
- 2 tbsp soy sauce
- 2 tbsp rice vinegar
- 1 tbsp sesame oil
- 1 tsp ginger, minced
- 1 tsp garlic, minced
- Sesame seeds and nori for garnish

Directions

1. Cook soba noodles according to package instructions.
2. In a pan, sauté shiitake mushrooms, carrots, and edamame.
3. In a bowl, whisk together soy sauce, rice vinegar, sesame oil, ginger, and garlic.
4. Toss cooked noodles in the sauce.
5. Divide noodles into bowls and top with sautéed veggies.
6. Garnish with green onions, sesame seeds, and nori.
Slurp away!

Substitutions

- Use spinach instead of shiitake mushrooms for a twist
- Tamari sauce can replace soy sauce

2 servings

320 calories

10 mins

Vegan Mediterranean Bowl

Ingredients:

- 1 cup cooked quinoa
- 1 cup cherry tomatoes, halved
- 1 cup cucumber, diced
- 1/2 cup Kalamata olives, pitted
- 1/4 cup red onion, thinly sliced
- 1/4 cup fresh parsley, chopped
- 2 tbsp olive oil
- 2 tbsp lemon juice
- 1 tsp dried oregano
- Salt and pepper to taste

A taste of the Mediterranean in a bowl! Fresh, healthy, and bursting with flavors from the sun-soaked region.

Directions

1. In a bowl, combine quinoa, cherry tomatoes, cucumber, olives, red onion, and parsley.
2. In a separate bowl, whisk together olive oil, lemon juice, oregano, salt, and pepper.
3. Drizzle the dressing over the quinoa mixture.
4. Toss to combine and serve.
Enjoy a taste of the Mediterranean!

Substitutions

- Add chickpeas for extra protein
- Feta cheese for a non-vegan twist

4
servings

420
calories

25 mins

Vegan Teriyaki Bowl

Ingredients:

- 2 cups cooked brown rice
- 2 cups broccoli florets
- 1 cup sliced bell peppers
- 1 cup sliced carrots
- 1 cup firm tofu, cubed
- 1/2 cup teriyaki sauce
- 2 tbsp vegetable oil
- Sesame seeds and green onions for garnish

Substitutions

- Use tempeh instead of tofu
- Add pineapple for a tropical twist

Sweet and savory perfection! This vegan teriyaki bowl is an explosion of Japanese flavors in every bite.

Directions

1. In a large skillet, heat vegetable oil over medium-high heat.
2. Add tofu cubes and cook until golden brown.
3. Remove tofu and set aside.
4. In the same skillet, stir-fry broccoli, bell peppers, and carrots until tender.
5. Add teriyaki sauce and tofu back to the skillet, stirring to coat.
6. Serve over cooked brown rice.
7. Garnish with sesame seeds and green onions. Enjoy the teriyaki magic!

3
servings

380
calories

30 mins

Vegan Bibimbap Bowl

Ingredients:

- 2 cups cooked short-grain rice
- 1 cup baby spinach
- 1 cup shredded carrots
- 1 cup bean sprouts
- 1 cup sliced cucumber
- 1 cup shiitake mushrooms, sliced
- 3 tbsp gochujang sauce
- 2 tbsp sesame oil
- 2 cloves garlic, minced
- 1 tsp sesame seeds
- Salt and pepper to taste

Substitutions

- Swap out vegetables based on your preferences
- Use a vegan kimchi for extra flavor

A Korean classic gone vegan! This bibimbap bowl is a colorful and satisfying mix of flavors and textures.

Directions

1. Divide cooked rice among bowls.
2. Saute spinach, carrots, bean sprouts, cucumber, and shiitake mushrooms separately.
3. In a small bowl, mix gochujang sauce, sesame oil, garlic, salt, and pepper.
4. Top rice with sautéed veggies.
5. Drizzle with the sauce.
6. Garnish with sesame seeds.
Enjoy your bibimbap masterpiece!

2
servings

380
calories

20 mins

Vegan BBQ Bowl

BBQ goodness without the meat! This vegan BBQ bowl is a smoky, saucy delight that'll satisfy your cravings.

Ingredients:

- 1 cup cooked quinoa
- 1 cup BBQ chickpeas (cooked with BBQ sauce)
- 1 cup corn on the cob, grilled and sliced
- 1 cup coleslaw (vegan mayo-based)
- 1/4 cup red onion, finely chopped
- 1/4 cup fresh cilantro, chopped
- Vegan BBQ sauce for drizzling

Directions

1. Cook quinoa according to package instructions.
2. In a skillet, heat BBQ chickpeas.
3. Grill corn and slice kernels off the cob.
4. Assemble bowls with quinoa, BBQ chickpeas, grilled corn, coleslaw, red onion, and cilantro.
5. Drizzle with vegan BBQ sauce.
Dig in and enjoy the BBQ goodness!

Substitutions

- Add avocado for creaminess
- Use store-bought vegan coleslaw for convenience

4
servings

350
calories

15 mins

Vegan Taco Bowl

Taco Tuesday, any day! This vegan taco bowl is a fiesta of flavors with a spicy kick and a whole lot of yum.

Ingredients:

- 2 cups cooked brown rice
- 1 cup black beans, canned and drained
- 1 cup corn kernels
- 1 cup diced tomatoes
- 1 cup shredded lettuce
- 1/2 cup red onion, finely chopped
- 1/4 cup fresh cilantro, chopped
- 1 lime, juiced
- 1 tbsp taco seasoning
- Salt and pepper to taste
- Vegan sour cream and salsa for garnish
- Tortilla chips for crunch

Directions

1. Cook brown rice according to package instructions.
2. In a skillet, warm black beans and corn over medium heat.
3. Mix in taco seasoning, salt, and pepper.
4. Assemble bowls with rice, bean mixture, tomatoes, lettuce, red onion, and cilantro.
5. Drizzle with lime juice.
6. Top with vegan sour cream and salsa.
7. Serve with tortilla chips.
Viva la fiesta!

Substitutions

- Use quinoa instead of brown rice
- Add sliced jalapeños for extra heat

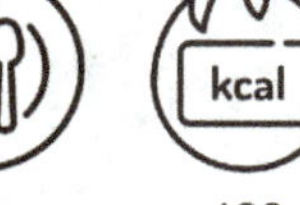

2
servings

420
calories

25 mins

Vegan Thai Bowl

A taste of Thailand in a bowl! This vegan Thai bowl is a harmony of sweet, sour, and spicy flavors.

Ingredients:

- 1 cup cooked jasmine rice
- 1 cup tofu, cubed and fried
- 1 cup mixed bell peppers, sliced
- 1 cup snap peas, trimmed
- 1/2 cup shredded carrots
- 1/4 cup fresh basil leaves
- 2 tbsp Thai sweet chili sauce
- 2 tbsp soy sauce
- 1 tbsp lime juice
- 1 tsp sriracha sauce (adjust to taste)
- Crushed peanuts and lime wedges for garnish

Directions

1. Cook jasmine rice according to package instructions.
2. Fry tofu until golden brown.
3. In a pan, stir-fry bell peppers, snap peas, and carrots until tender.
4. In a bowl, whisk together Thai sweet chili sauce, soy sauce, lime juice, and sriracha.
5. Toss tofu and veggies in the sauce.
6. Serve over cooked jasmine rice.
7. Garnish with basil leaves, crushed peanuts, and lime wedges.
Enjoy the Thai flavors!

Substitutions

- Use tempeh or seitan instead of tofu
- Add pineapple for sweetness

2
servings

320
calories

15 mins

Vegan Breakfast Bowl

Ingredients:

- 1 cup cooked oatmeal
- 1 cup mixed berries
- 1/2 cup almond yogurt
- 1/4 cup sliced almonds
- 2 tbsp maple syrup
- 1 tsp cinnamon
- Fresh mint leaves for garnish

Rise and shine! This vegan breakfast bowl is a nutritious and satisfying way to start your day with a smile.

Directions

1. Cook oatmeal according to package instructions.
2. Top oatmeal with mixed berries, almond yogurt, sliced almonds, maple syrup, and cinnamon.
3. Garnish with fresh mint leaves.
4. Enjoy your wholesome breakfast!

Substitutions

- Use Greek yogurt if not strictly vegan
- Drizzle with honey instead of maple syrup

3
servings

450
calories

20 mins

Vegan Power Bowl

Power up with this vegan bowl! Packed with protein and nutrients, it's the perfect fuel for an active day.

Ingredients:

- 2 cups cooked quinoa
- 1 cup chickpeas, roasted
- 1 cup kale, massaged and chopped
- 1 cup roasted sweet potato cubes
- 1/2 cup sliced radishes
- 1/4 cup pumpkin seeds
- 2 tbsp tahini dressing
- Salt and pepper to taste

Directions

1. Cook quinoa according to package instructions.
2. Roast chickpeas until crispy.
3. Massage kale with a bit of salt to soften.
4. Assemble bowls with quinoa, chickpeas, kale, sweet potato, radishes, and pumpkin seeds.
5. Drizzle with tahini dressing.
6. Season with salt and pepper.
Power up and conquer your day!

Substitutions

- Add grilled tofu for extra protein
- Use any preferred greens for kale

A small favor to ask

Hey there, my fellow culinary adventurers,

Let's pause for a moment in our exploration of the "Plant-Based Quick and Easy Cookbook: Fast, Healthy, and Delicious." We've journeyed through the realm of vibrant plant-based cuisine, embracing the art of crafting quick, wholesome, and utterly delectable meals. But before we get back to the recipes that make our taste buds dance with delight, I want to chat about something vital.

Reviews. Those elusive, shimmering gems of the publishing world. They're the lifeblood of any cookbook, especially one from a small, passionate team like ours. Each review you leave is like a secret spice that elevates our culinary creations to new heights.

Here's the deal, folks. Your opinions, your ratings, and those brief sentences you jot down are worth their weight in saffron. They help others discover the magic we've uncovered together in these pages, and they propel our culinary journey forward.

So, I'm kindly asking for your support. As we whip up, sauté, and savor the next delicious recipes, please take a moment to return to the app or platform from which you graciously welcomed this cookbook into your life. There, you'll find the review button, a humble tool waiting for your culinary wisdom.

Whether you write a sentence, a paragraph, or simply rate us with those shining stars, know that every review warms our hearts. In the world of artistic endeavors, perfection may be the goal, but it's often the imperfections that lend beauty to the craft. We've poured our souls into creating this cookbook, and while we've strived for excellence, a minor hiccup may sneak through the kitchen doors from time to time.

As a small, dedicated publisher, we rely on your feedback to keep the flame alive. So please, let your words become a beacon for others seeking delicious, plant-based fare. Share your experiences, your culinary triumphs, and even the occasional mishap. It all helps us grow and evolve.

Now, as you turn the pages and dive into the next incredible recipe, remember that your review is a vital ingredient in the ongoing saga of this cookbook. Your insights encourage others to savor the beauty of plant-based cuisine, and your words guide them on their culinary journey.

Thank you for being part of our flavorful adventure. Now, let's return to the recipes and keep creating magic together.

With boundless appreciation and a zest for culinary exploration,

Garden of Grapes

Chapter 5:
Simple and Flavorful Pasta

4
servings

350
calories

30 mins

Vegan Spaghetti Bolognese

A hearty classic made vegan! This spaghetti bolognese is rich, savory, and perfect for a comforting meal.

Ingredients:

- 8 oz spaghetti
- 1 cup lentils, cooked and drained
- 1 cup tomato sauce
- 1/2 cup diced onion
- 1/2 cup diced carrots
- 1/2 cup diced celery
- 2 cloves garlic, minced
- 1 tsp olive oil
- 1 tsp dried oregano
- 1 tsp dried basil
- Salt and pepper to taste
- Fresh basil leaves for garnish

Directions

1. Cook spaghetti according to package instructions.
2. In a pan, heat olive oil and sauté onion, carrots, celery, and garlic until softened.
3. Add cooked lentils, tomato sauce, oregano, basil, salt, and pepper.
4. Simmer for 15 minutes.
5. Serve sauce over cooked spaghetti.
6. Garnish with fresh basil.
Enjoy your vegan comfort food!

Substitutions

- Use any pasta of your choice
- Substitute lentils with textured vegetable protein for a meatier texture

4 servings

380 calories

20 mins

Creamy Vegan Alfredo

Indulge in creamy goodness! This vegan alfredo pasta is luxuriously silky and satisfying, without the dairy.

Ingredients:

- 8 oz fettuccine pasta
- 1 cup cashews, soaked and drained
- 1 cup unsweetened almond milk
- 2 cloves garlic, minced
- 2 tbsp nutritional yeast
- 2 tbsp lemon juice
- 2 tbsp olive oil
- Salt and pepper to taste
- Fresh parsley for garnish

Directions

1. Cook fettuccine pasta according to package instructions.
2. In a blender, combine soaked cashews, almond milk, garlic, nutritional yeast, lemon juice, olive oil, salt, and pepper.
3. Blend until creamy.
4. Toss cooked pasta with the alfredo sauce.
5. Garnish with fresh parsley.
Indulge and savor the creamy delight!

Substitutions

- Use any pasta shape you like
- Substitute cashews with blanched almonds for a different flavor

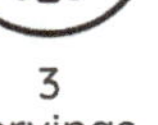

3
servings

320
calories

15 mins

Vegan Pesto Pasta

Ingredients:

- 8 oz penne pasta
- 2 cups fresh basil leaves
- 1/2 cup pine nuts
- 1/4 cup nutritional yeast
- 2 cloves garlic, minced
- 1/4 cup olive oil
- 2 tbsp lemon juice
- Salt and pepper to taste
- Cherry tomatoes and fresh basil for garnish

Fresh and fragrant! This vegan pesto pasta is a burst of green goodness that's simple yet incredibly flavorful.

Directions

1. Cook penne pasta according to package instructions.
2. In a food processor, combine basil, pine nuts, nutritional yeast, garlic, olive oil, lemon juice, salt, and pepper.
3. Blend into a smooth pesto sauce.
4. Toss cooked pasta with the pesto.
5. Garnish with cherry tomatoes and fresh basil leaves.
Enjoy the fresh flavors!

Substitutions

- Use any pasta shape you prefer
- Swap pine nuts for walnuts or almonds

6
servings

420
calories

45 mins

Vegan Lasagna

Layers of comfort! This vegan lasagna is a timeless classic made with layers of rich tomato sauce and creamy tofu.

Ingredients:

- 9 lasagna noodles, cooked
- 2 cups marinara sauce
- 1 cup firm tofu, crumbled
- 1 cup spinach, chopped
- 1/2 cup shredded vegan mozzarella cheese
- 1/4 cup nutritional yeast
- 2 cloves garlic, minced
- 1 tsp dried oregano
- Salt and pepper to taste
- Fresh basil for garnish

Directions

1. Preheat oven to 350°F (175°C).
2. In a bowl, combine crumbled tofu, spinach, nutritional yeast, garlic, oregano, salt, and pepper.
3. In a baking dish, layer marinara sauce, lasagna noodles, tofu mixture, and vegan mozzarella.
4. Repeat the layers.
5. Bake for 30 minutes.
6. Garnish with fresh basil.
Dig into layers of deliciousness!

Substitutions

- Use gluten-free lasagna noodles if needed
- Add your favorite veggies to the tofu mixture

4 servings

400 calories

25 mins

Vegan Carbonara

Ingredients:

- 8 oz spaghetti
- 1 cup cashews, soaked and drained
- 1 cup unsweetened almond milk
- 1/2 cup frozen peas
- 1/4 cup vegan bacon bits
- 2 cloves garlic, minced
- 2 tbsp nutritional yeast
- 2 tbsp olive oil
- Salt and pepper to taste
- Fresh parsley for garnish

Substitutions

- Use any pasta shape you like
- Substitute vegan bacon bits with sautéed mushrooms for a different flavor

Creamy and comforting! This vegan carbonara is a dreamy pasta dish with a luscious cashew-based sauce.

Directions

1. Cook spaghetti according to package instructions.
2. In a blender, combine soaked cashews, almond milk, frozen peas, vegan bacon bits, garlic, nutritional yeast, olive oil, salt, and pepper.
3. Blend until creamy.
4. Toss cooked pasta with the carbonara sauce.
5. Garnish with fresh parsley.
Savor the creamy delight!

4
servings

350
calories

20 mins

Spicy Peanut Noodles

A flavor explosion! These spicy peanut noodles are a zesty and satisfying treat with a kick of heat.

Ingredients:

- 8 oz udon noodles
- 1/2 cup peanut butter
- 1/4 cup soy sauce
- 2 tbsp rice vinegar
- 2 tbsp maple syrup
- 1 tbsp sriracha sauce (adjust to taste)
- 1 clove garlic, minced
- 1 tsp ginger, minced
- 1/2 cup chopped scallions
- 1/4 cup chopped peanuts
- Lime wedges for garnish

Directions

1. Cook udon noodles according to package instructions.
2. In a bowl, whisk together peanut butter, soy sauce, rice vinegar, maple syrup, sriracha sauce, garlic, and ginger.
3. Toss cooked noodles with the peanut sauce.
4. Garnish with scallions, chopped peanuts, and lime wedges.
Get ready for a spicy delight!

Substitutions

- Use any noodles you prefer
- Adjust the level of sriracha for your preferred spice level

4
servings

380
calories

25 mins

Vegan Mac and Cheese

Ingredients:

- 8 oz elbow macaroni
- 1 cup raw cashews, soaked and drained
- 1 cup unsweetened almond milk
- 1/2 cup nutritional yeast
- 2 cloves garlic, minced
- 2 tbsp lemon juice
- 1 tsp Dijon mustard
- Salt and pepper to taste
- Paprika for garnish

Childhood favorite, all grown up! This vegan mac and cheese is creamy, cheesy, and utterly satisfying.

Directions

1. Cook macaroni according to package instructions.
2. In a blender, combine soaked cashews, almond milk, nutritional yeast, garlic, lemon juice, Dijon mustard, salt, and pepper.
3. Blend until creamy.
4. Toss cooked macaroni with the cheese sauce.
5. Sprinkle with paprika.
Enjoy the creamy nostalgia!

Substitutions

- Use any pasta shape you like
- Add roasted broccoli for extra veggies

3 servings

320 calories

20 mins

Vegan Lemon Asparagus Pasta

Light and zesty! This vegan lemon asparagus pasta is a refreshing delight with a citrusy kick and tender asparagus.

Ingredients:

- 8 oz linguine
- 1 cup asparagus spears, trimmed and cut into pieces
- 1/4 cup olive oil
- 2 cloves garlic, minced
- Zest and juice of 1 lemon
- 1/4 cup chopped fresh basil
- Salt and pepper to taste
- Lemon slices for garnish

Directions

1. Cook linguine according to package instructions.
2. In a pan, sauté asparagus and garlic in olive oil until tender.
3. Add lemon zest and juice, fresh basil, salt, and pepper.
4. Toss cooked linguine with the asparagus mixture
5. Garnish with lemon slices.
Enjoy the refreshing flavors!

Substitutions

- Use any pasta shape you prefer
- Add cherry tomatoes for extra color and flavor

4
servings

420
calories

30 mins

Creamy and earthy! This vegan mushroom risotto is a luscious comfort dish that's perfect for mushroom lovers.

Vegan Mushroom Risotto

Ingredients:

- 1 cup Arborio rice
- 1 cup sliced mushrooms
- 1/2 cup diced onion
- 2 cloves garlic, minced
- 4 cups vegetable broth
- 1/4 cup white wine (optional)
- 2 tbsp olive oil
- 2 tbsp nutritional yeast
- 1 tbsp fresh thyme leaves
- Salt and pepper to taste
- Fresh parsley for garnish

Directions

1. In a large skillet, heat olive oil and sauté onion, garlic, and mushrooms until soft.
2. Add Arborio rice and cook for 2 minutes.
3. Pour in white wine (if using) and cook until mostly absorbed.
4. Gradually add vegetable broth, one cup at a time, stirring frequently until absorbed.
5. Stir in nutritional yeast, fresh thyme, salt, and pepper.
6. Cook until rice is creamy and tender.
7. Garnish with fresh parsley.
Enjoy the creamy mushroom goodness!

Substitutions

- Use any type of mushrooms you like
- Replace white wine with vegetable broth

2
servings

280
calories

15 mins

Vegan Zucchini Noodles with Pesto

Ingredients:

- 2 large zucchinis, spiralized into noodles
- 1 cup cherry tomatoes, halved
- 1/4 cup vegan pesto
- 2 tbsp pine nuts
- 1 tbsp nutritional yeast
- Salt and pepper to taste

Light and refreshing! These vegan zucchini noodles are paired with fresh pesto for a healthy and flavorful dish.

Directions

1. Spiralize zucchinis into noodles.
2. In a large bowl, toss zucchini noodles with cherry tomatoes, vegan pesto, pine nuts, nutritional yeast, salt, and pepper.
3. Serve chilled.
Enjoy a light and healthy meal!

Substitutions

- Add sliced black olives for extra flavor
- Top with vegan Parmesan cheese if desired

Chapter 6:
Comforting Classics

4
servings

320
calories

45 mins

Vegan Stuffed Peppers

Classic comfort! These vegan stuffed peppers are filled with a savory mixture and baked to perfection.

Ingredients:

- 4 bell peppers
- 1 cup cooked quinoa
- 1 cup black beans, canned and drained
- 1 cup corn kernels
- 1 cup diced tomatoes
- 1/2 cup diced onion
- 2 cloves garlic, minced
- 1 tsp chili powder
- 1 tsp cumin
- Salt and pepper to taste
- Vegan cheese for topping
- Fresh cilantro for garnish

Directions

1. Preheat the oven to 350°F (175°C).
2. Cut the tops off the bell peppers and remove seeds and membranes.
3. In a large bowl, mix together quinoa, black beans, corn, diced tomatoes, onion, garlic, chili powder, cumin, salt, and pepper.
4. Stuff the mixture into the bell peppers.
5. Place the peppers in a baking dish and cover with foil.
6. Bake for 30-35 minutes, until the peppers are tender.
7. Remove the foil, top with vegan cheese, and bake for an additional 5 minutes, until the cheese is melted and bubbly.
8. Garnish with fresh cilantro.
Enjoy the comforting goodness!

Substitutions

- Use brown rice instead of quinoa
- Add your favorite veggies to the stuffing mix

6
servings

350
calories

45 mins

Vegan Meatloaf

Ingredients:

- 2 cups cooked lentils
- 1 cup rolled oats
- 1 cup diced onion
- 1/2 cup diced celery
- 1/2 cup diced carrots
- 2 cloves garlic, minced
- 1/4 cup tomato sauce
- 2 tbsp soy sauce
- 1 tbsp vegan Worcestershire sauce
- 1 tsp dried thyme
- Salt and pepper to taste
- Ketchup or BBQ sauce for glazing

Substitutions

- Use chickpeas or black beans instead of lentils
- Customize the glaze with your favorite sauce

A vegan twist on a classic! This vegan meatloaf is hearty, savory, and perfect for a cozy family dinner.

Directions

1. Preheat the oven to 350°F (175°C).
2. In a food processor, pulse cooked lentils until partially mashed.
3. In a large bowl, combine mashed lentils, rolled oats, diced onion, celery, carrots, garlic, tomato sauce, soy sauce, vegan Worcestershire sauce, dried thyme, salt, and pepper.
4. Press the mixture into a greased loaf pan.
5. Bake for 30 minutes.
6. Brush the top with ketchup or BBQ sauce.
7. Bake for an additional 15 minutes, until firm and browned.
8. Let it cool for a few minutes before slicing. Enjoy the vegan comfort!

4
servings

380
calories

30 mins

Vegan BBQ Ribs

Ingredients:

- 2 cups vital wheat gluten flour
- 1/4 cup nutritional yeast
- 1 tsp smoked paprika
- 1 tsp garlic powder
- 1 tsp onion powder
- 1 cup vegetable broth
- 1/4 cup tomato paste
- 1/4 cup BBQ sauce
- 2 tbsp soy sauce
- 1 tsp liquid smoke (optional)
- Salt and pepper to taste
- BBQ sauce for basting and serving

Substitutions

- Customize the BBQ sauce to your liking
- Grill on a stovetop grill pan or in the oven

Finger-licking goodness! These vegan BBQ ribs are made with seitan and smothered in barbecue sauce.

Directions

1. In a large bowl, mix vital wheat gluten flour, nutritional yeast, smoked paprika, garlic powder, and onion powder.
2. In a separate bowl, whisk together vegetable broth, tomato paste, BBQ sauce, soy sauce, liquid smoke (if using), salt, and pepper.
3. Pour the wet ingredients into the dry ingredients and mix until it forms a dough.
4. Knead the dough for a few minutes.
5. Shape the dough into rib-like shapes.
6. Heat a grill or grill pan over medium-high heat.
7. Grill the ribs for about 5-7 minutes on each side, basting with BBQ sauce.
8. Serve with extra BBQ sauce.
Enjoy the smoky goodness!

4
servings

180
calories

30 mins

Vegan Buffalo Cauliflower Wings

Ingredients:

- 1 head cauliflower, cut into florets
- 1 cup almond milk
- 1 cup all-purpose flour
- 1 tsp garlic powder
- 1 tsp onion powder
- 1/2 cup hot sauce
- 2 tbsp vegan butter, melted
- 1 tbsp maple syrup
- Salt and pepper to taste
- Vegan ranch or blue cheese dressing for dipping

Substitutions

- Adjust the level of hot sauce for your preferred spice level
- Use gluten-free flour for a gluten-free version

Spicy and addictive! These vegan buffalo cauliflower wings are the perfect appetizer or game-day snack.

Directions

1. Preheat the oven to 450°F (230°C).
2. In a bowl, whisk together almond milk, flour, garlic powder, onion powder, salt, and pepper to make the batter.
3. Dip cauliflower florets into the batter and place them on a baking sheet.
4. Bake for 20-25 minutes, until crispy and golden.
5. In another bowl, mix hot sauce, melted vegan butter, maple syrup, salt, and pepper to make the buffalo sauce.
6. Toss the baked cauliflower in the buffalo sauce until coated.
7. Serve with vegan ranch or blue cheese dressing.
Get ready for some spicy goodness!

 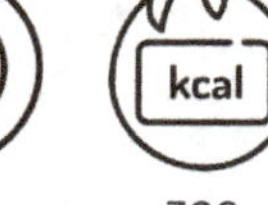 

**4
servings**

**320
calories**

25 mins

Vegan Sloppy Joes

Ingredients:

- 1 cup lentils, cooked and drained
- 1 cup diced bell peppers
- 1/2 cup diced onion
- 1/2 cup diced celery
- 1/2 cup tomato sauce
- 2 tbsp tomato paste
- 2 tbsp maple syrup
- 1 tbsp soy sauce
- 1 tsp chili powder
- Salt and pepper to taste
- Vegan burger buns or bread of choice

Substitutions

- Customize the spice level with more or less chili powder
- Add pickles or coleslaw for extra flavor

Messy and delicious! These vegan sloppy joes are a saucy and satisfying twist on a classic sandwich.

Directions

1. In a skillet, sauté diced bell peppers, onion, and celery until softened.
2. Add cooked lentils, tomato sauce, tomato paste, maple syrup, soy sauce, chili powder, salt, and pepper.
3. Simmer for 10-15 minutes, until the mixture thickens.
4. Serve on vegan burger buns.
Enjoy the saucy mess!

4
servings

320
calories

20 mins

Vegan Quesadillas

Cheesy goodness! These vegan quesadillas are filled with savory vegetables and vegan cheese, perfect for a quick meal.

Ingredients:

- 4 large tortillas
- 1 cup vegan cheese shreds
- 1 cup black beans, canned and drained
- 1 cup diced bell peppers
- 1/2 cup diced onion
- 1/2 cup diced tomatoes
- 1/4 cup fresh cilantro, chopped
- 2 tsp olive oil
- Guacamole and salsa for serving

Directions

1. In a skillet, heat olive oil and sauté diced bell peppers and onion until softened.
2. Place a tortilla in the skillet and sprinkle with vegan cheese.
3. Add black beans, sautéed bell peppers and onion, diced tomatoes, and fresh cilantro on one half of the tortilla.
4. Fold the other half over to create a half-moon shape.
5. Cook on both sides until golden and crispy.
6. Repeat for the remaining tortillas.
7. Serve with guacamole and salsa.
Enjoy the cheesy goodness!

Substitutions

- Customize the filling with your favorite veggies
- Use vegan sour cream for dipping

4
servings

380
calories

35 mins

Vegan Meatball Subs

Ingredients:

- 4 sub rolls
- 12 vegan meatballs (store-bought or homemade)
- 2 cups marinara sauce
- 1 cup vegan mozzarella cheese shreds
- Fresh basil leaves for garnish

Substitutions

- Make your own vegan meatballs using lentils or mushrooms
- Add sautéed bell peppers and onions for extra flavor

Hearty and satisfying! These vegan meatball subs are loaded with savory meatballs, marinara sauce, and vegan cheese.

Directions

1. Preheat the oven to 375°F (190°C).
2. Bake vegan meatballs according to package instructions.
3. In a saucepan, heat marinara sauce.
4. Place cooked meatballs in the sauce and simmer for a few minutes.
5. Slice sub rolls and place vegan meatballs and sauce inside.
6. Sprinkle with vegan mozzarella cheese shreds.
7. Bake subs for a few minutes until the cheese is melted and rolls are toasted.
8. Garnish with fresh basil leaves.
Enjoy the hearty goodness!

4 servings

380 calories

30 mins

Vegan Philly Cheesesteak

Ingredients:

- 4 sub rolls
- 2 cups sliced seitan
- 1 cup sliced bell peppers
- 1 cup sliced onions
- 1 cup vegan provolone cheese slices
- 2 tbsp olive oil
- Salt and pepper to taste

Philly classic gone vegan! This vegan Philly cheesesteak is loaded with savory seitan, peppers, onions, and vegan cheese.

Directions

1. Heat olive oil in a skillet over medium heat.
2. Add sliced seitan, bell peppers, and onions.
3. Sauté until seitan is heated through and veggies are tender.
4. Season with salt and pepper.
5. Slice sub rolls and place seitan, peppers, and onions inside.
6. Top with vegan provolone cheese slices.
7. Heat in the oven until the cheese is melted and rolls are toasted.
8. Serve hot.
Enjoy the Philly classic!

Substitutions

- Customize with your favorite veggies
- Use vegan cheese of your choice

4
servings

360
calories

20 mins

Vegan Reuben Sandwiches

Ingredients:

- 8 slices rye bread
- 2 cups sliced seitan pastrami
- 1 cup sauerkraut, drained
- 1/2 cup vegan Russian dressing
- 8 slices vegan Swiss cheese (optional)
- Vegan butter for toasting

Substitutions

- Customize with your favorite vegan deli meats
- Use vegan mayonnaise instead of Russian dressing

Deli-style delight! These vegan Reuben sandwiches feature hearty seitan pastrami, sauerkraut, and Russian dressing.

Directions

1. Spread vegan Russian dressing on one side of each slice of rye bread.
2. On half of the slices, layer seitan pastrami, sauerkraut, and vegan Swiss cheese (if using).
3. Top with the remaining slices of bread, dressing side down.
4. Heat a skillet over medium heat and spread vegan butter on the outside of each sandwich.
5. Grill sandwiches until the bread is toasted and the cheese (if using) is melted.
6. Slice and serve hot.
Enjoy the deli-style delight!

Chapter 7:
Fresh and Vibrant Salads

4
servings

320
calories

20 mins

Vegan Cobb Salad

Ingredients:

- 8 cups mixed greens
- 1 cup cherry tomatoes, halved
- 1 cup cucumber, diced
- 1 cup corn kernels, fresh or frozen
- 1 cup diced avocado
- 1 cup smoky tempeh bacon, crumbled
- 1/2 cup diced red onion
- 1/4 cup vegan ranch dressing
- Salt and pepper to taste

A salad with a rainbow of flavors! This vegan Cobb salad is packed with fresh veggies, avocado, and smoky tempeh bacon for a satisfying meal.

Directions

1. In a large salad bowl, arrange mixed greens.
2. Layer cherry tomatoes, cucumber, corn kernels, avocado, smoky tempeh bacon, and red onion on top.
3. Drizzle with vegan ranch dressing.
4. Season with salt and pepper.
5. Toss the salad just before serving.
Enjoy the rainbow of flavors!

Substitutions

- Customize with your favorite veggies
- Use your preferred vegan dressing

4
servings

280
calories

15 mins

Vegan Caprese Salad

Ingredients:

- 4 large tomatoes, sliced
- 1 cup fresh basil leaves
- 1 cup vegan mozzarella cheese, sliced
- 2 tbsp balsamic glaze
- 2 tbsp extra-virgin olive oil
- Salt and pepper to taste

A taste of Italy! This vegan Caprese salad features ripe tomatoes, fresh basil, and creamy vegan mozzarella drizzled with balsamic glaze.

Directions

1. Arrange tomato slices, fresh basil leaves, and vegan mozzarella cheese on a platter.
2. Drizzle with balsamic glaze and extra-virgin olive oil.
3. Season with salt and pepper.
4. Serve immediately.
Enjoy the Italian flavors!

Substitutions

- Use heirloom tomatoes for a colorful twist
- Make your own vegan mozzarella cheese

4
servings

320
calories

20 mins

Vegan Waldorf Salad

Ingredients:

- 4 cups mixed greens
- 2 cups diced apples
- 1 cup diced celery
- 1 cup red grapes, halved
- 1/2 cup chopped walnuts
- 1/4 cup vegan mayonnaise
- 1/4 cup plain vegan yogurt
- 2 tbsp maple syrup
- 1 tsp lemon juice
- Salt and pepper to taste

Substitutions

- Use your favorite variety of apple
- Add dried cranberries for extra sweetness

A classic with a twist! This vegan Waldorf salad combines crisp apples, celery, grapes, and walnuts in a creamy vegan dressing.

Directions

1. In a large salad bowl, arrange mixed greens.
2. Combine diced apples, diced celery, red grapes, and chopped walnuts in a separate bowl.
3. In another bowl, whisk together vegan mayonnaise, plain vegan yogurt, maple syrup, lemon juice, salt, and pepper to make the dressing.
4. Pour the dressing over the apple mixture and toss to coat.
5. Spoon the apple mixture over the mixed greens.
6. Serve immediately.
Enjoy the creamy twist on a classic!

4
servings

180
calories

15 mins

Vegan Watermelon Salad

Ingredients:

- 4 cups cubed watermelon
- 1 cup diced cucumber
- 1/4 cup fresh mint leaves, chopped
- 2 tbsp lime juice
- 1 tbsp agave syrup or maple syrup
- 1/4 tsp chili powder (optional)
- Salt to taste

Substitutions

- Add crumbled vegan feta cheese for a savory twist
- Garnish with lime zest for extra zing

Sweet and refreshing! This vegan watermelon salad combines juicy watermelon with mint, cucumber, and a tangy lime dressing for a burst of summer flavors.

Directions

1. In a large salad bowl, combine cubed watermelon, diced cucumber, and chopped fresh mint leaves.
2. In a small bowl, whisk together lime juice, agave syrup or maple syrup, chili powder (if using), and a pinch of salt to make the dressing.
3. Drizzle the dressing over the watermelon mixture.
4. Toss gently to coat.
5. Serve immediately.
Enjoy the summer sweetness!

4 servings · **260 calories** · **20 mins**

Vegan Caesar Salad

Ingredients:

- 8 cups chopped romaine lettuce
- 2 cups garlic croutons (store-bought or homemade)
- 1/4 cup vegan Caesar dressing
- 1/4 cup vegan Parmesan cheese
- Lemon wedges for garnish
- Salt and pepper to taste

Substitutions

- Make your own croutons with your preferred bread
- Customize with your favorite vegan protein

Creamy and savory! This vegan Caesar salad features crisp romaine lettuce, garlicky croutons, and a dairy-free Caesar dressing.

Directions

1. In a large salad bowl, place chopped romaine lettuce.
2. Top with garlic croutons.
3. Drizzle with vegan Caesar dressing.
4. Sprinkle vegan Parmesan cheese on top.
5. Season with salt and pepper.
6. Serve with lemon wedges for an extra zing.
Enjoy the creamy Caesar goodness!

4
servings

280
calories

15 mins

Vegan Greek Salad

Ingredients:

- 4 cups diced cucumbers
- 2 cups diced tomatoes
- 1/2 cup sliced red onion
- 1/2 cup Kalamata olives, pitted
- 1/2 cup vegan feta cheese, crumbled
- 1/4 cup fresh parsley, chopped
- 2 tbsp extra-virgin olive oil
- 2 tbsp red wine vinegar
- 1 tsp dried oregano
- Salt and pepper to taste

Substitutions

- Customize with your favorite Mediterranean veggies
- Make your own vegan feta cheese

Mediterranean delight! This vegan Greek salad is bursting with cucumbers, tomatoes, olives, and vegan feta cheese, all dressed in a zesty vinaigrette.

Directions

1. In a large salad bowl, combine diced cucumbers, diced tomatoes, sliced red onion, Kalamata olives, vegan feta cheese, and fresh parsley.
2. In a small bowl, whisk together extra-virgin olive oil, red wine vinegar, dried oregano, salt, and pepper to make the vinaigrette.
3. Drizzle the vinaigrette over the salad.
4. Toss gently to coat.
5. Serve immediately.
Enjoy the Mediterranean flavors!

4 servings · **320 calories** · **20 mins**

Vegan Southwestern Salad

Ingredients:

- 8 cups mixed greens
- 1 cup black beans, canned and drained
- 1 cup corn kernels, fresh or frozen
- 1 cup diced avocado
- 1/2 cup diced red onion
- 1/4 cup chopped fresh cilantro
- 2 tbsp extra-virgin olive oil
- 2 tbsp lime juice
- 1 tsp ground cumin
- Salt and pepper to taste

A fiesta in a bowl! This vegan Southwestern salad features black beans, corn, avocado, and a zesty cilantro-lime dressing.

Directions

1. In a large salad bowl, arrange mixed greens.
2. Layer black beans, corn kernels, diced avocado, red onion, and fresh cilantro on top.
3. In a small bowl, whisk together extra-virgin olive oil, lime juice, ground cumin, salt, and pepper to make the dressing.
4. Drizzle the dressing over the salad.
5. Toss gently to coat.
6. Serve immediately.
Enjoy the Southwestern fiesta!

Substitutions

- Add diced jalapeños for extra heat
- Top with vegan sour cream or salsa

4
servings

240
calories

20 mins

Vegan Asian Slaw

Ingredients:

- 6 cups shredded cabbage (green and red)
- 1 cup shredded carrots
- 1 cup sliced bell peppers (red, yellow, or orange)
- 1/4 cup chopped scallions
- 1/4 cup chopped fresh cilantro
- 2 tbsp sesame seeds
- 2 tbsp sesame oil
- 2 tbsp rice vinegar
- 1 tbsp soy sauce
- 1 tbsp maple syrup
- 1 tsp grated ginger
- Salt and pepper to taste

Substitutions

- Add sliced almonds or chopped peanuts for extra crunch
- Customize with your favorite veggies

Crunchy and flavorful! This vegan Asian slaw combines cabbage, carrots, and bell peppers in a sesame ginger dressing for a delightful side dish.

Directions

1. In a large bowl, combine shredded cabbage, shredded carrots, sliced bell peppers, chopped scallions, chopped fresh cilantro, and sesame seeds.
2. In a small bowl, whisk together sesame oil, rice vinegar, soy sauce, maple syrup, grated ginger, salt, and pepper to make the dressing.
3. Drizzle the dressing over the slaw.
4. Toss gently to coat.
5. Serve immediately.
Enjoy the crunchy Asian flavors!

4
servings

280
calories

20 mins

Vegan Broccoli Salad

Ingredients:

- 4 cups broccoli florets, blanched and cooled
- 1/2 cup raisins
- 1/2 cup sunflower seeds
- 1/4 cup diced red onion
- 1/4 cup vegan mayonnaise
- 1/4 cup plain vegan yogurt
- 2 tbsp apple cider vinegar
- 1 tbsp maple syrup
- Salt and pepper to taste

Substitutions

- Add diced apples or grapes for extra sweetness
- Customize with your favorite nuts

Creamy and satisfying! This vegan broccoli salad features crisp broccoli florets, raisins, and a tangy vegan dressing.

Directions

1. In a large salad bowl, combine blanched and cooled broccoli florets, raisins, sunflower seeds, and diced red onion.
2. In a small bowl, whisk together vegan mayonnaise, plain vegan yogurt, apple cider vinegar, maple syrup, salt, and pepper to make the dressing.
3. Drizzle the dressing over the salad.
4. Toss gently to coat.
5. Serve immediately.
Enjoy the creamy broccoli goodness!

4
servings

240
calories

15 mins

Vegan Kale Salad with Lemon Tahini Dressing

Easy

Ingredients:

- 8 cups chopped kale leaves (stems removed)
- 1 cup cooked chickpeas, canned and drained
- 1/2 cup cherry tomatoes, halved
- 1/4 cup diced red onion
- 2 tbsp hemp seeds
- 2 tbsp lemon tahini dressing
- Juice of 1 lemon
- Salt and pepper to taste

Nutrient-packed! This vegan kale salad features hearty kale leaves, chickpeas, and a zesty lemon tahini dressing for a healthy and satisfying meal.

Directions

1. In a large salad bowl, place chopped kale leaves.
2. Add cooked chickpeas, cherry tomatoes, diced red onion, and hemp seeds.
3. Drizzle with lemon tahini dressing and the juice of 1 lemon.
4. Season with salt and pepper.
5. Massage the kale for a few minutes to tenderize it.
6. Serve immediately.
Enjoy the nutrient-packed goodness!

Substitutions

- Add avocado slices for creaminess
- Customize with your favorite beans or legumes

Chapter 8: Wholesome Soups and Stews

6 servings

220 calories

30 mins

Vegan Minestrone Soup

Ingredients:

- 2 tbsp olive oil
- 1 cup diced onion
- 1/2 cup diced carrots
- 1/2 cup diced celery
- 2 cloves garlic, minced
- 1 can (14 oz) diced tomatoes
- 1 can (14 oz) kidney beans, drained and rinsed
- 1 can (14 oz) cannellini beans, drained and rinsed
- 6 cups vegetable broth
- 1 cup small pasta (e.g., ditalini or elbow)
- 2 cups chopped spinach or kale
- 1 tsp dried basil
- 1 tsp dried oregano
- Salt and pepper to taste

Substitutions

- Customize with your favorite veggies
- Use your preferred pasta shape

Hearty Italian goodness! This vegan minestrone soup is brimming with vegetables, beans, and pasta.

Directions

1. In a large pot, heat olive oil over medium heat.
2. Sauté diced onion, diced carrots, diced celery, and minced garlic until softened.
3. Add diced tomatoes, kidney beans, cannellini beans, vegetable broth, small pasta, dried basil, and dried oregano.
4. Bring to a boil, then reduce heat and simmer for 15-20 minutes, until pasta is tender.
5. Stir in chopped spinach or kale and cook until wilted.
6. Season with salt and pepper.
7. Serve hot.
Enjoy the hearty Italian flavors!

4
servings

180
calories

25 mins

Vegan Tomato Basil Soup

Ingredients:

- 2 tbsp olive oil
- 1 cup diced onion
- 2 cloves garlic, minced
- 2 cans (28 oz each) diced tomatoes
- 1 cup vegetable broth
- 1/2 cup fresh basil leaves
- 1/4 cup coconut milk (or any non-dairy milk)
- Salt and pepper to taste

Substitutions

- Garnish with croutons or vegan Parmesan cheese
- Use canned tomato puree for a smoother texture

Classic comfort! This vegan tomato basil soup is silky, smooth, and bursting with the flavors of ripe tomatoes and fresh basil.

Directions

1. In a large pot, heat olive oil over medium heat.
2. Sauté diced onion and minced garlic until softened.
3. Add diced tomatoes (with their juices) and vegetable broth.
4. Bring to a simmer and cook for 15 minutes.
5. Stir in fresh basil leaves.
6. Use an immersion blender to blend the soup until smooth.
7. Return the soup to the pot and stir in coconut milk.
8. Season with salt and pepper.
9. Reheat if needed and serve hot.
Enjoy the classic comfort!

4
servings

280
calories

30 mins

Vegan Potato Leek Soup

Ingredients:

- 2 tbsp olive oil
- 2 leeks, white and light green parts, sliced
- 4 cups diced potatoes
- 4 cups vegetable broth
- 1 cup unsweetened almond milk (or any non-dairy milk)
- 2 cloves garlic, minced
- 1 tsp dried thyme
- Salt and pepper to taste

Substitutions

- Garnish with fresh chives or parsley
- Use russet or Yukon Gold potatoes for creaminess

Creamy and comforting! This vegan potato leek soup is velvety smooth and perfect for chilly days.

Directions

1. In a large pot, heat olive oil over medium heat.
2. Sauté sliced leeks and minced garlic until softened.
3. Add diced potatoes, vegetable broth, dried thyme, salt, and pepper.
4. Bring to a boil, then reduce heat and simmer for 20-25 minutes, until potatoes are tender.
5. Use an immersion blender to blend the soup until smooth.
6. Return the soup to the pot and stir in almond milk.
7. Reheat if needed and serve hot.
Enjoy the creamy comfort!

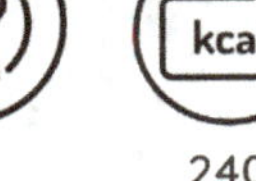

6
servings

240
calories

35 mins

Vegan Lentil Soup

Ingredients:

- 2 tbsp olive oil
- 1 cup diced onion
- 1/2 cup diced carrots
- 1/2 cup diced celery
- 2 cloves garlic, minced
- 1 cup dried green or brown lentils, rinsed and drained
- 6 cups vegetable broth
- 1 can (14 oz) diced tomatoes
- 1 tsp ground cumin
- 1/2 tsp ground coriander
- 1/2 tsp smoked paprika
- Salt and pepper to taste

Protein-packed! This vegan lentil soup is hearty and wholesome, featuring lentils, vegetables, and aromatic spices.

Directions

1. In a large pot, heat olive oil over medium heat.
2. Sauté diced onion, diced carrots, diced celery, and minced garlic until softened.
3. Add dried lentils, vegetable broth, diced tomatoes, ground cumin, ground coriander, smoked paprika, salt, and pepper.
4. Bring to a boil, then reduce heat and simmer for 25-30 minutes, until lentils are tender.
5. Serve hot.
Enjoy the protein-packed goodness!

Substitutions

- Add diced potatoes or spinach for extra nutrients
- Customize with your favorite spices

4
servings

220
calories

30 mins

Vegan Butternut Squash Soup

Ingredients:

- 2 tbsp olive oil
- 1 butternut squash, peeled, seeded, and diced
- 1 cup diced onion
- 2 cloves garlic, minced
- 4 cups vegetable broth
- 1/2 cup unsweetened coconut milk (or any non-dairy milk)
- 1/2 tsp ground nutmeg
- Salt and pepper to taste

Substitutions

- Garnish with a drizzle of maple syrup or a sprinkle of cinnamon
- Use canned butternut squash puree for convenience

Autumn delight! This vegan butternut squash soup is velvety, sweet, and seasoned with a hint of nutmeg.

Directions

1. In a large pot, heat olive oil over medium heat.
2. Sauté diced onion and minced garlic until softened.
3. Add diced butternut squash, vegetable broth, ground nutmeg, salt, and pepper.
4. Bring to a boil, then reduce heat and simmer for 20-25 minutes, until squash is tender.
5. Use an immersion blender to blend the soup until smooth.
6. Return the soup to the pot and stir in coconut milk.
7. Reheat if needed and serve hot.
Enjoy the autumn delight!

6
servings

320
calories

40 mins

Vegan Gumbo

Ingredients:

- 1/4 cup vegetable oil
- 1/4 cup all-purpose flour
- 1 cup diced onion
- 1/2 cup diced bell peppers (green, red, or yellow)
- 1/2 cup diced celery
- 2 cloves garlic, minced
- 1 cup sliced okra (fresh or frozen)
- 1 can (14 oz) diced tomatoes
- 4 cups vegetable broth
- 1 cup sliced vegan sausage (e.g., andouille or smoked)
- 1 cup cooked red kidney beans, drained and rinsed
- 1 tsp dried thyme
- 1 tsp dried oregano
- 1/2 tsp smoked paprika
- 1/4 tsp cayenne pepper (adjust to taste)
- Salt and pepper to taste

Substitutions

- Customize with your favorite vegetables and protein
- Adjust the spice level to your preference

Creole comfort! This vegan gumbo is rich and flavorful, featuring a roux, okra, and a medley of vegetables.

Directions

1. In a large pot, heat vegetable oil over medium heat to make the roux.
2. Add all-purpose flour and stir constantly until the roux turns brown (similar to peanut butter in color).
3. Add diced onion, diced bell peppers, diced celery, and minced garlic to the roux.
4. Sauté until the vegetables are softened.
5. Stir in sliced okra, diced tomatoes, vegetable broth, sliced vegan sausage, cooked red kidney beans, dried thyme, dried oregano, smoked paprika, cayenne pepper, salt, and pepper.
6. Bring to a boil, then reduce heat and simmer for 15-20 minutes.
7. Serve hot.
Enjoy the Creole comfort!

4
servings

160
calories

25 mins

Easy

Vegan Mushroom Soup

Ingredients:

- 2 tbsp olive oil
- 1 cup diced onion
- 2 cups sliced mushrooms (any variety)
- 2 cloves garlic, minced
- 4 cups vegetable broth
- 1 cup unsweetened almond milk (or any non-dairy milk)
- 2 tbsp all-purpose flour
- 1 tsp dried thyme
- Salt and pepper to taste

Substitutions

- Garnish with fresh parsley or chives
- Use a mix of wild mushrooms for depth of flavor

Earthy elegance! This vegan mushroom soup is rich, creamy, and showcases the earthy flavors of mushrooms.

Directions

1. In a large pot, heat olive oil over medium heat.
2. Sauté diced onion until softened.
3. Add sliced mushrooms and minced garlic, and sauté until mushrooms are tender.
4. Stir in all-purpose flour and dried thyme to create a roux.
5. Gradually add vegetable broth and unsweetened almond milk while stirring to avoid lumps.
6. Bring to a boil, then reduce heat and simmer for 15-20 minutes.
7. Season with salt and pepper.
8. Serve hot.
Enjoy the earthy elegance!

4
servings

300
calories

30 mins

Vegan Thai Coconut Soup

Ingredients:

- 2 tbsp vegetable oil
- 1 cup diced onion
- 2 cloves garlic, minced
- 2 tbsp red curry paste
- 4 cups vegetable broth
- 1 can (14 oz) coconut milk
- 1 cup sliced mushrooms
- 1 cup diced tofu
- 1 cup sliced bell peppers (red or yellow)
- 1 cup baby corn, halved
- 2 tbsp soy sauce
- 1 tbsp brown sugar
- Juice of 1 lime
- Fresh cilantro leaves for garnish
- Thai basil leaves for garnish (optional)
- Thai red chilies for garnish (optional)
- Salt to taste

Substitutions

- Customize the spice level with more or less red curry paste
- Add your favorite vegetables or protein

Thai-inspired comfort! This vegan Thai coconut soup is aromatic and creamy, with a perfect balance of sweet and spicy.

Directions

1. In a large pot, heat vegetable oil over medium heat.
2. Sauté diced onion until softened.
3. Add minced garlic and red curry paste, and sauté for 1-2 minutes until fragrant.
4. Stir in vegetable broth and coconut milk.
5. Add sliced mushrooms, diced tofu, sliced bell peppers, and baby corn.
6. Bring to a simmer and cook for 10-15 minutes, until vegetables are tender.
7. Season with soy sauce, brown sugar, lime juice, and salt.
8. Serve hot, garnished with fresh cilantro leaves, Thai basil leaves, and Thai red chilies if desired.
Enjoy the Thai-inspired comfort!

6
servings

240
calories

35 mins

Vegan Black Bean Soup

Ingredients:

- 2 tbsp vegetable oil
- 1 cup diced onion
- 1/2 cup diced bell peppers (green or red)
- 1/2 cup diced celery
- 2 cloves garlic, minced
- 3 cans (15 oz each) black beans, drained and rinsed
- 4 cups vegetable broth
- 1 can (14 oz) diced tomatoes
- 1 tsp chili powder
- 1/2 tsp ground cumin
- 1/2 tsp smoked paprika
- Salt and pepper to taste

Substitutions

- Top with vegan sour cream, avocado, or cilantro
- Customize with your favorite toppings

Southwestern flair! This vegan black bean soup is hearty, smoky, and loaded with black beans and spices.

Directions

1. In a large pot, heat vegetable oil over medium heat.
2. Sauté diced onion, diced bell peppers, diced celery, and minced garlic until softened.
3. Add two cans of black beans, vegetable broth, diced tomatoes, chili powder, ground cumin, smoked paprika, salt, and pepper.
4. Bring to a boil, then reduce heat and simmer for 15-20 minutes.
5. Use an immersion blender to blend the soup until partially smooth, leaving some texture.
6. Stir in the remaining can of black beans for added texture.
7. Serve hot.
Enjoy the Southwestern flair!

6
servings

280
calories

40 mins

Vegan Split Pea Soup

Ingredients:

- 2 tbsp olive oil
- 1 cup diced onion
- 1/2 cup diced carrots
- 1/2 cup diced celery
- 2 cloves garlic, minced
- 2 cups green split peas, rinsed and drained
- 8 cups vegetable broth
- 1 bay leaf
- 1 tsp dried thyme
- 1/2 tsp dried marjoram
- Salt and pepper to taste

Substitutions

- Garnish with fresh parsley or croutons
- Add diced potatoes or ham-style tempeh for extra heartiness

Old-fashioned comfort! This vegan split pea soup is thick, hearty, and seasoned with herbs and spices.

Directions

1. In a large pot, heat olive oil over medium heat.
2. Sauté diced onion, diced carrots, diced celery, and minced garlic until softened.
3. Add green split peas, vegetable broth, bay leaf, dried thyme, dried marjoram, salt, and pepper.
4. Bring to a boil, then reduce heat and simmer for 30-35 minutes, until split peas are tender.
5. Remove the bay leaf.
6. Use an immersion blender to partially blend the soup, leaving some texture.
7. Serve hot.
Enjoy the old-fashioned comfort!

Chapter 9:
One-Pot Wonders

4 servings

380 calories

45 mins

Vegan Paella

Ingredients:

- 2 tbsp olive oil
- 1 cup diced onion
- 1 cup diced bell peppers (red and green)
- 1 cup diced tomatoes
- 2 cloves garlic, minced
- 1 1/2 cups Arborio rice
- 4 cups vegetable broth
- 1 tsp smoked paprika
- 1/2 tsp saffron threads (optional)
- 1 can (15 oz) chickpeas, drained and rinsed
- 1 cup frozen peas
- Lemon wedges for garnish
- Salt and pepper to taste

Substitutions

- Customize with your favorite vegetables
- Substitute saffron with turmeric for color
- Use any preferred protein

Spanish delight! This vegan paella is a flavorful medley of saffron-infused rice, vegetables, and protein-rich chickpeas.

Directions

1. In a large paella pan or skillet, heat olive oil over medium heat.
2. Sauté diced onion, diced bell peppers, and minced garlic until softened.
3. Add diced tomatoes and cook for a few minutes.
4. Stir in Arborio rice, vegetable broth, smoked paprika, and saffron threads (if using).
5. Bring to a simmer and cook for 20-25 minutes, stirring occasionally, until rice is tender and has absorbed the liquid.
6. Add chickpeas and frozen peas, and cook for an additional 5 minutes.
7. Season with salt and pepper.
8. Serve hot with lemon wedges for garnish. Enjoy the Spanish delight!

6
servings

280
calories

30 mins

Vegan Quinoa Chili

Ingredients:

- 2 tbsp olive oil
- 1 cup diced onion
- 1/2 cup diced bell peppers (green or red)
- 2 cloves garlic, minced
- 1 cup quinoa, rinsed and drained
- 2 cans (15 oz each) black beans, drained and rinsed
- 1 can (14 oz) diced tomatoes
- 4 cups vegetable broth
- 2 tsp chili powder
- 1 tsp ground cumin
- 1/2 tsp smoked paprika
- Salt and pepper to taste

Substitutions

- Top with vegan sour cream, avocado, or vegan cheese
- Customize with your favorite toppings

Protein-packed! This vegan quinoa chili is hearty and satisfying, filled with quinoa, beans, and smoky spices.

Directions

1. In a large pot, heat olive oil over medium heat.
2. Sauté diced onion, diced bell peppers, and minced garlic until softened.
3. Add quinoa, black beans, diced tomatoes, vegetable broth, chili powder, ground cumin, smoked paprika, salt, and pepper.
4. Bring to a boil, then reduce heat and simmer for 20-25 minutes, until quinoa is cooked and chili thickens.
5. Serve hot.
Enjoy the protein-packed goodness!

4
servings

180
calories

30 mins

Vegan Ratatouille

Ingredients:

- 2 tbsp olive oil
- 1 cup diced onion
- 2 cloves garlic, minced
- 1 cup diced eggplant
- 1 cup diced zucchini
- 1 cup diced bell peppers (red and green)
- 1 cup diced tomatoes
- 1 can (14 oz) crushed tomatoes
- 1 tsp dried thyme
- 1 tsp dried rosemary
- Salt and pepper to taste

Substitutions

- Garnish with fresh basil or parsley
- Customize with your favorite herbs

French elegance! This vegan ratatouille is a colorful medley of summer vegetables, slow-cooked to perfection in tomato sauce.

Directions

1. In a large skillet, heat olive oil over medium heat.
2. Sauté diced onion and minced garlic until softened.
3. Add diced eggplant, diced zucchini, and diced bell peppers.
4. Cook for 5-7 minutes until vegetables start to soften.
5. Stir in diced tomatoes, crushed tomatoes, dried thyme, dried rosemary, salt, and pepper.
6. Cover and simmer for 15-20 minutes, until vegetables are tender.
7. Serve hot.
Enjoy the French elegance!

4
servings

320
calories

35 mins

Vegan Sweet Potato Curry

Ingredients:

- 2 tbsp vegetable oil
- 1 cup diced onion
- 2 cloves garlic, minced
- 1 cup diced sweet potatoes
- 1 can (15 oz) chickpeas, drained and rinsed
- 1 can (14 oz) diced tomatoes
- 1 can (14 oz) coconut milk
- 2 tsp curry powder
- 1 tsp ground turmeric
- 1/2 tsp ground cumin
- Salt and pepper to taste

Substitutions

- Garnish with fresh cilantro or toasted coconut flakes
- Customize with your favorite vegetables

Creamy and comforting! This vegan sweet potato curry features tender sweet potatoes, chickpeas, and aromatic spices in a luscious coconut milk sauce.

Directions

1. In a large skillet, heat vegetable oil over medium heat.
2. Sauté diced onion and minced garlic until softened.
3. Add diced sweet potatoes, chickpeas, diced tomatoes, coconut milk, curry powder, ground turmeric, ground cumin, salt, and pepper.
4. Bring to a simmer and cook for 20-25 minutes, until sweet potatoes are tender and curry thickens.
5. Serve hot.
Enjoy the creamy comfort!

4
servings

240
calories

25 mins

Vegan Teriyaki Stir-Fry

Ingredients:

- 2 tbsp vegetable oil
- 1 block (14 oz) extra-firm tofu, cubed
- 1 cup broccoli florets
- 1 cup sliced bell peppers (red, yellow, or green)
- 1 cup sliced carrots
- 1/2 cup sliced snow peas
- 1/4 cup teriyaki sauce (store-bought or homemade)
- Cooked rice or noodles for serving
- Sesame seeds and sliced green onions for garnish (optional)
- Salt and pepper to taste

Substitutions

- Customize with your favorite vegetables and protein
- Adjust the sweetness and saltiness of the teriyaki sauce to your preference

Asian fusion! This vegan teriyaki stir-fry is a delicious combination of tofu, colorful vegetables, and a sweet and savory teriyaki sauce.

Directions

1. In a large wok or skillet, heat vegetable oil over medium-high heat.
2. Add cubed tofu and stir-fry until golden brown and slightly crispy.
3. Transfer tofu to a plate and set aside.
4. In the same wok, add broccoli florets, sliced bell peppers, sliced carrots, and sliced snow peas.
5. Stir-fry for 5-7 minutes until vegetables are tender-crisp.
6. Return the tofu to the wok.
7. Pour teriyaki sauce over the tofu and vegetables.
8. Cook for an additional 2-3 minutes, stirring to coat everything in the sauce.
9. Season with salt and pepper.
10. Serve hot over cooked rice or noodles. Enjoy the Asian fusion!

4
servings

280
calories

40 mins

Vegan Lemon Herb Risotto

Ingredients:

- 2 tbsp olive oil
- 1 cup Arborio rice
- 1/2 cup diced onion
- 2 cloves garlic, minced
- Zest and juice of 1 lemon
- 4 cups vegetable broth
- 1/2 cup dry white wine (optional)
- 2 tbsp chopped fresh parsley
- 1 tbsp chopped fresh basil
- 1 tbsp chopped fresh thyme
- Salt and pepper to taste

Substitutions

- Garnish with extra lemon zest and fresh herbs
- Customize with your favorite herbs

Elegant and zesty! This vegan lemon herb risotto is creamy, fragrant, and infused with the flavors of fresh herbs and citrus.

Directions

1. In a large saucepan, heat olive oil over medium heat.
2. Sauté diced onion and minced garlic until softened.
3. Stir in Arborio rice and cook for 1-2 minutes until lightly toasted.
4. Add lemon zest and juice, and stir.
5. Gradually add vegetable broth and dry white wine (if using), one ladle at a time, stirring frequently until the liquid is absorbed before adding more.
6. Continue this process for about 20-25 minutes, until the rice is creamy and tender.
7. Stir in chopped fresh parsley, chopped fresh basil, and chopped fresh thyme.
8. Season with salt and pepper.
9. Serve hot.
Enjoy the elegant and zesty flavors!

4
servings

220
calories

30 mins.

Vegan Mexican Rice

Ingredients:

- 2 tbsp vegetable oil
- 1 cup long-grain white rice
- 1/2 cup diced onion
- 1/2 cup diced bell peppers (red or green)
- 2 cloves garlic, minced
- 1 can (14 oz) diced tomatoes
- 2 cups vegetable broth
- 1 tsp chili powder
- 1/2 tsp cumin powder
- Salt and pepper to taste

Substitutions

- Garnish with fresh cilantro or lime wedges
- Customize with your preferred level of spiciness

Fiery and flavorful! This vegan Mexican rice is a spicy side dish with tomatoes, bell peppers, and a kick of chili powder.

Directions

1. In a large skillet, heat vegetable oil over medium heat.
2. Add long-grain white rice and sauté until lightly golden.
3. Stir in diced onion, diced bell peppers, and minced garlic until softened.
4. Add diced tomatoes, vegetable broth, chili powder, cumin powder, salt, and pepper.
5. Bring to a boil, then reduce heat and simmer for 20-25 minutes, until rice is cooked and liquid is absorbed.
6. Fluff the rice with a fork.
7. Serve hot.
Enjoy the fiery and flavorful side!

4 servings · **180 calories** · **25 mins**

Vegan Cauliflower Fried Rice

Ingredients:

- 2 tbsp vegetable oil
- 1 head cauliflower, riced (or 4 cups store-bought cauliflower rice)
- 1/2 cup diced onion
- 1/2 cup diced carrots
- 1/2 cup frozen peas
- 1/2 cup diced bell peppers (red or green)
- 2 cloves garlic, minced
- 2 tbsp soy sauce (or tamari for gluten-free)
- 1 tsp sesame oil
- 1/2 tsp ginger powder
- Salt and pepper to taste

Substitutions

- Customize with your favorite vegetables and protein
- Add a dash of sriracha for extra heat

Low-carb delight! This vegan cauliflower fried rice is a healthier alternative to traditional fried rice, with cauliflower rice and an array of veggies.

Directions

1. In a large skillet, heat vegetable oil over medium-high heat.
2. Add riced cauliflower and sauté for 5-7 minutes until it begins to soften.
3. Stir in diced onion, diced carrots, frozen peas, diced bell peppers, and minced garlic.
4. Cook for an additional 5-7 minutes until vegetables are tender-crisp.
5. Drizzle soy sauce, sesame oil, and ginger powder over the cauliflower mixture.
6. Stir to combine and cook for 2-3 more minutes.
7. Season with salt and pepper.
8. Serve hot.
Enjoy the low-carb delight!

4
servings

260
calories

30 mins

Vegan Chickpea and Spinach Curry

Ingredients:

- 2 tbsp vegetable oil
- 1 cup diced onion
- 2 cloves garlic, minced
- 1 can (15 oz) chickpeas, drained and rinsed
- 2 cups chopped spinach
- 1 can (14 oz) diced tomatoes
- 1 can (14 oz) coconut milk
- 2 tsp curry powder
- 1 tsp ground cumin
- 1/2 tsp ground coriander
- Salt and pepper to taste

Substitutions

- Garnish with fresh cilantro or a squeeze of lime
- Customize with your preferred level of spiciness

Indian-inspired comfort! This vegan chickpea and spinach curry is rich and flavorful, with tender chickpeas and a creamy tomato-based sauce.

Directions

1. In a large skillet, heat vegetable oil over medium heat.
2. Sauté diced onion and minced garlic until softened.
3. Add chickpeas, chopped spinach, diced tomatoes, coconut milk, curry powder, ground cumin, ground coriander, salt, and pepper.
4. Bring to a simmer and cook for 15-20 minutes, allowing the flavors to meld together.
5. Serve hot.
Enjoy the Indian-inspired comfort!

4
servings

320
calories

20 mins

Vegan Lemon Garlic Pasta

Ingredients:

- 8 oz linguine or your favorite pasta
- 2 tbsp olive oil
- 4 cloves garlic, minced
- Zest and juice of 1 lemon
- 1/4 cup chopped fresh parsley
- 1/4 cup chopped fresh basil
- Salt and pepper to taste

Substitutions

- Garnish with vegan Parmesan cheese or nutritional yeast
- Customize with your favorite herbs

Bright and zesty! This vegan lemon garlic pasta is a quick and flavorful dish with a tangy lemon and garlic sauce.

Directions

1. Cook pasta according to package instructions until al dente.
2. In a skillet, heat olive oil over medium heat.
3. Add minced garlic and sauté for 1-2 minutes until fragrant.
4. Stir in lemon zest, lemon juice, chopped fresh parsley, and chopped fresh basil.
5. Season with salt and pepper.
6. Drain cooked pasta and add it to the skillet with the lemon garlic sauce.
7. Toss to coat the pasta.
8. Serve hot.
Enjoy the bright and zesty flavors!

Chapter 10: Savory Sandwiches and Wraps

2
servings

350
calories

40 mins

Vegan Falafel Wrap

Ingredients:

- 4 store-bought or homemade falafel patties
- 2 whole wheat pita bread
- 1 cup shredded lettuce
- 1/2 cup diced tomatoes
- 1/2 cup diced cucumbers
- 1/4 cup diced red onion
- 1/4 cup chopped fresh parsley
- 1/4 cup tahini sauce
- Juice of 1 lemon
- Salt and pepper to taste

Substitutions

- Customize with your favorite veggies
- Make your own falafel from scratch

Middle Eastern delight! This vegan falafel wrap is a flavorful combination of crispy falafel, fresh veggies, and creamy tahini sauce, all wrapped in warm pita bread.

Directions

1. Cook falafel patties according to package instructions until crispy and golden brown.
2. Warm pita bread in a dry skillet or oven.
3. In a small bowl, mix tahini sauce with lemon juice, salt, and pepper.
4. Assemble the wraps: Place a pita bread on a clean surface.
5. Place 2 falafel patties in the center of each pita.
6. Top with shredded lettuce, diced tomatoes, diced cucumbers, diced red onion, and chopped fresh parsley.
7. Drizzle with tahini sauce.
8. Fold in the sides of the pita and roll it up tightly.
9. Serve hot.
Enjoy the Middle Eastern delight!

2 servings

380 calories

25 mins

Vegan Banh Mi Sandwich

Ingredients:

- 1 baguette or French bread
- 8 oz extra-firm tofu, sliced and pressed
- 1/4 cup soy sauce or tamari
- 2 tbsp rice vinegar
- 2 tbsp maple syrup
- 1 clove garlic, minced
- 1 cup shredded carrots
- 1 cup sliced cucumbers
- 1/4 cup thinly sliced red onion
- 1/4 cup chopped fresh cilantro
- 2 tbsp vegan sriracha mayo (or mix vegan mayo with sriracha)
- Salt and pepper to taste

Substitutions

- Customize with your favorite pickled veggies
- Adjust the spiciness with more or less sriracha mayo

Vietnamese fusion! This vegan Banh Mi sandwich features marinated tofu, crisp pickled vegetables, and a kick of spicy sriracha mayo, all in a baguette.

Directions

1. In a bowl, whisk together soy sauce, rice vinegar, maple syrup, and minced garlic.
2. Marinate tofu slices in the mixture for 15-20 minutes.
3. In a separate bowl, combine shredded carrots, sliced cucumbers, thinly sliced red onion, and chopped fresh cilantro.
4. Preheat a grill pan or skillet over medium-high heat.
5. Grill marinated tofu slices for 2-3 minutes on each side until grill marks appear.
6. Slice the baguette into two sandwich-sized pieces and toast them.
7. Assemble the sandwiches: Spread sriracha mayo on both sides of the baguette.
8. Place grilled tofu slices on the bottom half of the baguette.
9. Top with the vegetable mixture.
10. Season with salt and pepper.
11. Close the sandwich with the top half of the baguette.
12. Serve hot or wrap in foil for later.
Enjoy the Vietnamese fusion!

2 servings

280 calories

30 mins

Vegan Portobello Mushroom Burger

Hearty and satisfying! This vegan Portobello mushroom burger is a juicy and flavorful sandwich with marinated mushrooms, fresh greens, and a creamy sauce on a whole-grain bun.

Ingredients:

- 2 whole-grain burger buns
- 2 large Portobello mushrooms, stems removed
- 1/4 cup balsamic vinegar
- 2 tbsp olive oil
- 2 cloves garlic, minced
- 1 tsp dried thyme
- Salt and pepper to taste
- 2 cups mixed greens (e.g., spinach, arugula, or lettuce)
- 1/4 cup vegan mayo
- 2 tsp Dijon mustard
- 1 tsp lemon juice
- 2 tomato slices
- 1/4 cup red onion rings

Substitutions

- Customize with your favorite greens and toppings
- Use your preferred burger buns

Directions

1. In a bowl, whisk together balsamic vinegar, olive oil, minced garlic, dried thyme, salt, and pepper.
2. Place Portobello mushrooms in a shallow dish and pour the marinade over them.
3. Marinate for 15-20 minutes, turning the mushrooms occasionally.
4. Preheat a grill or grill pan over medium-high heat.
5. Grill Portobello mushrooms for 3-4 minutes on each side until tender.
6. While mushrooms cook, mix vegan mayo, Dijon mustard, and lemon juice in a small bowl.
7. Toast the whole-grain burger buns.
8. Assemble the burgers: Spread the creamy sauce on both halves of the buns.
9. Place a grilled Portobello mushroom on the bottom half of each bun.
10. Top with mixed greens, tomato slices, and red onion rings.
11. Close the burger with the top half of the bun.
12. Serve hot.
Enjoy the hearty and satisfying burger!

2 servings

350 calories

30 mins

Vegan Tempeh Reuben

Ingredients:

- 4 slices rye bread
- 8 oz tempeh, sliced
- 1/4 cup vegetable broth
- 2 tbsp soy sauce or tamari
- 1 tsp liquid smoke (optional)
- 1/2 cup sauerkraut, drained
- 4 slices vegan Swiss cheese
- 1/4 cup Russian dressing (store-bought or homemade)
- Pickle spears for serving (optional)
- Salt and pepper to taste

Substitutions

- Customize with your favorite condiments and toppings
- Use your preferred bread

Classic comfort! This vegan Tempeh Reuben sandwich features marinated tempeh, sauerkraut, vegan Swiss cheese, and Russian dressing on rye bread.

Directions

1. In a bowl, whisk together vegetable broth, soy sauce, and liquid smoke (if using).
2. Marinate tempeh slices in the mixture for 15-20 minutes.
3. Preheat a skillet over medium-high heat.
4. Sauté marinated tempeh slices for 2-3 minutes on each side until golden brown.
5. Toast rye bread slices.
6. Assemble the sandwiches: Spread Russian dressing on two slices of rye bread.
7. Layer tempeh slices on top of the dressing.
8. Add sauerkraut and vegan Swiss cheese slices.
9. Season with salt and pepper.
10. Close the sandwiches with the remaining rye bread slices.
11. Serve hot with pickle spears if desired. Enjoy the classic comfort!

2 servings

320 calories

20 mins

Vegan Caprese Panini

Ingredients:

- 1 ciabatta loaf or 4 ciabatta rolls
- 2 ripe tomatoes, thinly sliced
- 1 cup fresh basil leaves
- 4 slices vegan mozzarella cheese
- Balsamic glaze (store-bought or homemade)
- Olive oil for grilling
- Salt and pepper to taste

Substitutions

- Customize with your favorite vegan cheese
- Add a drizzle of olive oil before grilling

Italian elegance! This vegan Caprese panini is a delightful combination of ripe tomatoes, fresh basil, vegan mozzarella, and balsamic glaze, all grilled to perfection in ciabatta bread.

Directions

1. Preheat a panini press or grill pan.
2. Slice the ciabatta loaf or rolls in half and brush the inside with olive oil.
3. Assemble the paninis: On the bottom half of each ciabatta piece, layer tomato slices, fresh basil leaves, and vegan mozzarella slices.
4. Drizzle balsamic glaze over the toppings.
5. Season with salt and pepper.
6. Top with the remaining ciabatta halves.
7. Place the paninis on the panini press or grill pan and cook according to the manufacturer's instructions until golden brown and the cheese is melted.
8. Serve hot.
Enjoy the Italian elegance!

2
servings

260
calories

35 mins

Vegan Buffalo Cauliflower Wrap

Ingredients:

- 2 large tortillas (whole wheat or your choice)
- 2 cups cauliflower florets
- 2 tbsp olive oil
- 1/4 cup Buffalo sauce (store-bought or homemade)
- 1/2 cup diced avocado
- 1/4 cup vegan ranch dressing (store-bought or homemade)
- 1/4 cup shredded lettuce
- 1/4 cup diced celery
- Salt and pepper to taste

Substitutions

- Customize with your favorite veggies and greens
- Adjust the spiciness with more or less Buffalo sauce

Spicy and satisfying! This vegan Buffalo cauliflower wrap features crispy cauliflower bites, creamy avocado, and a spicy Buffalo sauce, all wrapped in a tortilla.

Directions

1. Preheat the oven to 425°F (220°C).
2. Toss cauliflower florets with olive oil, salt, and pepper on a baking sheet.
3. Roast for 25-30 minutes, flipping halfway, until cauliflower is crispy and browned.
4. In a bowl, toss roasted cauliflower with Buffalo sauce until coated.
5. Warm tortillas in a dry skillet or microwave.
6. Assemble the wraps: Spread vegan ranch dressing on each tortilla.
7. Place a portion of Buffalo cauliflower on top.
8. Add diced avocado, shredded lettuce, and diced celery.
9. Season with salt and pepper.
10. Fold in the sides of the tortilla and roll it up tightly.
11. Serve hot.
Enjoy the spicy and satisfying wrap!

2
servings

320
calories

35 mins

Vegan BBQ Pulled Jackfruit Sandwich

Ingredients:

- 2 whole-grain burger buns
- 1 can (20 oz) young green jackfruit in water or brine, drained and shredded
- 1/2 cup barbecue sauce (store-bought or homemade)
- 1 cup vegan coleslaw (store-bought or homemade)
- 4 pickle slices
- Olive oil for grilling
- Salt and pepper to taste

Substitutions

- Customize with your preferred barbecue sauce
- Add jalapeño slices for extra heat

Smoky and savory! This vegan BBQ pulled jackfruit sandwich features tender jackfruit in smoky barbecue sauce, piled high on a bun with coleslaw and pickles.

Directions

1. In a skillet, heat olive oil over medium-high heat.
2. Add shredded jackfruit and sauté for 3-4 minutes to remove excess moisture.
3. Pour barbecue sauce over the jackfruit and stir to coat.
4. Cook for an additional 5-7 minutes until jackfruit is tender and fully coated in sauce.
5. Toast whole-grain burger buns.
6. Assemble the sandwiches: Place a portion of BBQ pulled jackfruit on the bottom half of each bun.
7. Top with vegan coleslaw and pickle slices.
8. Season with salt and pepper.
9. Close the sandwiches with the top half of the buns.
10. Serve hot.
Enjoy the smoky and savory goodness!

2 servings

320 calories

20 mins

Vegan Mediterranean Wrap

Ingredients:

- 2 large tortillas (whole wheat or your choice)
- 1 cup hummus (store-bought or homemade)
- 1 cup roasted vegetables (e.g., bell peppers, zucchini, eggplant)
- 1/4 cup sliced Kalamata olives
- 1/4 cup chopped fresh parsley
- 1/4 cup diced red onion
- Juice of 1 lemon
- Olive oil for drizzling
- Salt and pepper to taste

Mediterranean delight! This vegan Mediterranean wrap is bursting with the flavors of hummus, roasted vegetables, olives, and fresh herbs, all wrapped in a soft tortilla.

Directions

1. Warm tortillas in a dry skillet or microwave.
2. Spread a generous layer of hummus on each tortilla.
3. Add roasted vegetables, sliced Kalamata olives, chopped fresh parsley, and diced red onion on top of the hummus.
4. Drizzle with olive oil and lemon juice.
5. Season with salt and pepper.
6. Fold in the sides of the tortilla and roll it up tightly.
7. Serve hot.
Enjoy the Mediterranean delight!

Substitutions

- Customize with your favorite roasted veggies
- Add a sprinkle of crumbled vegan feta cheese

2
servings

280
calories

30 mins

Vegan Tofu Banh Mi

Ingredients:

- 1 baguette or French bread
- 8 oz extra-firm tofu, sliced and pressed
- 1/4 cup soy sauce or tamari
- 2 tbsp rice vinegar
- 2 tbsp maple syrup
- 1 clove garlic, minced
- 1 cup shredded carrots
- 1 cup sliced cucumbers
- 1/4 cup thinly sliced red onion
- 1/4 cup chopped fresh cilantro
- 2 tbsp vegan sriracha mayo (or mix vegan mayo with sriracha)
- Salt and pepper to taste

Substitutions

- Customize with your favorite pickled veggies
- Adjust the spiciness with more or less sriracha mayo

Vietnamese fusion! This vegan tofu Banh Mi features marinated tofu, crisp pickled vegetables, and a kick of spicy sriracha mayo, all in a baguette.

Directions

1. In a bowl, whisk together soy sauce, rice vinegar, maple syrup, and minced garlic.
2. Marinate tofu slices in the mixture for 15-20 minutes.
3. In a separate bowl, combine shredded carrots, sliced cucumbers, thinly sliced red onion, and chopped fresh cilantro.
4. Preheat a grill pan or skillet over medium-high heat.
5. Grill marinated tofu slices for 2-3 minutes on each side until grill marks appear.
6. Slice the baguette into two sandwich-sized pieces and toast them.
7. Assemble the sandwiches: Spread sriracha mayo on both sides of the baguette.
8. Place grilled tofu slices on the bottom half of the baguette.
9. Top with the vegetable mixture.
10. Season with salt and pepper.
11. Close the sandwich with the top half of the baguette.
12. Serve hot or wrap in foil for later.
Enjoy the Vietnamese fusion!

2 servings

290 calories

20 mins

Vegan Chickpea Salad Wrap

Ingredients:

- 2 large tortillas (whole wheat or your choice)
- 1 can (15 oz) chickpeas, drained and rinsed
- 1/4 cup diced red bell pepper
- 1/4 cup diced celery
- 1/4 cup diced cucumber
- 1/4 cup diced red onion
- 1/4 cup chopped fresh parsley
- 1/4 cup chopped fresh dill
- 1/4 cup vegan mayo
- 1 tbsp Dijon mustard
- 1 tsp lemon juice
- Salt and pepper to taste

Substitutions

- Customize with your favorite veggies and herbs
- Add hot sauce for extra heat

Wholesome and satisfying! This vegan chickpea salad wrap features a flavorful chickpea salad with veggies, herbs, and a creamy dressing, all wrapped in a tortilla.

Directions

1. In a bowl, mash chickpeas with a fork or potato masher until partially mashed.
2. Add diced red bell pepper, diced celery, diced cucumber, diced red onion, chopped fresh parsley, and chopped fresh dill to the mashed chickpeas.
3. In a separate bowl, mix vegan mayo, Dijon mustard, lemon juice, salt, and pepper.
4. Combine the dressing with the chickpea salad and stir until well coated.
5. Warm tortillas in a dry skillet or microwave.
6. Assemble the wraps: Spoon chickpea salad onto each tortilla.
7. Roll up the tortilla, folding in the sides as you go.
8. Serve hot.
Enjoy the wholesome and satisfying wrap!

A small favor to ask

Dear Plant-Based Culinary Enthusiasts,

As we prepare to wrap up our plant-based culinary journey through the pages of "Plant-Based Quick and Easy Cookbook: Fast, Healthy, and Delicious," I want to express my deepest gratitude for taking the time to explore the vibrant world of plant-based cooking with us. This cookbook is a labor of love, and it brings me great joy to know that it has found a place in your kitchen, creating delectable and nourishing meals.

But before we part ways, I would like to ask a small favor from you, one that carries immense importance for a small, dedicated publishing team like ours. Reviews are the lifeblood of our work, and they are the compass that guides us in this culinary journey. Your feedback, your thoughts, and your experiences are invaluable to us.

If our recipes have allowed you to whip up a speedy, healthy, and delicious plant-based meal when you needed it most, then I kindly request your support. Your insights can encourage others to embrace plant-based cooking and savor the magic of flavors born from the earth.

Taking a moment to visit the platform or app where you acquired this cookbook, you will find the review button waiting for your input. A simple star rating and a few words to share your culinary adventures can make a world of difference. Your review can be the inspiration that someone needs to make a positive change in their life through plant-based cuisine.

Please understand that each review, no matter how succinct or detailed, is a source of inspiration for us. In the art of cooking, just like in life, small hiccups and occasional mistakes can occur. We've put our utmost effort into creating a cookbook that simplifies plant-based cooking, and your feedback can help us continue to refine our craft.

As you savor the fruits of your culinary adventures, please consider leaving a review. Reviews are a gift that keeps on giving, helping us to grow and inspire others in their quest for healthy, flavorful, and sustainable living.

I extend my heartfelt appreciation for choosing "Plant-Based Quick and Easy Cookbook." Your support not only fuels our passion for creating, but it also strengthens our resolve to spread the goodness of plant-based cuisine.

Thank you for being a cherished part of our culinary journey, and here's to the continuing exploration of fast, healthy, and delicious plant-based cooking.

With warm regards and heartfelt thanks,
Garden of Grapes